Guide to the
Catacombs
OF ROME

Introduction by *Umberto M. Fasola*
Text by *Fabrizio Mancinelli*

SCALA

1

TABLE OF CONTENTS

1. Crossing the Red Sea,
Catacomb of Via Latina.

3

INTRODUCTION

The illustrations for this book were collected by the late Professor Enrico Josi towards the end of a long and active life. The dissemination of knowledge about ancient Christian monuments – popularization in the higher sense of the term – formed an essential part of the professor's work, for he believed in the importance of these monuments as "venerable and authentic evidence of the faith and religious life of antiquity, and primary source material for the study of Christian institutions and culture", to use the words of Pope Plus XI. He wrote articles, clear, comprehensible and brimming with details, for the *Osservatore Romano* and other newspapers, and dedicated the last years of his life to reorganizing the collections of the Museo Cristiano e Profano Lateranense (the Lateran Museum) in their new lodgings in the Vatican. It was the ordinary visitor rather than the specialist that Professor Josi had in mind when he arranged the material for display in the new light-filled halls of the Vatican.

Thus, the sarcophagi and other sculptures were exhibited according to their subject matter, many casts were included of works exhibited elsewhere, and the great accomplishment of Giovan Battista De Rossi during XIX century – the organization of the vast epigraphical collection along pedogogical lines – was left intact. As a result, an attentive visitor can easily grasp the essential aspects of the art, organization, beliefs and mentality of the Christians of the first centuries AD.

This book has the same popularizing aim. In its preparation Professor Josi deliberately brought together all the most characteristic pictures of the catacombs and other cult buildings, in order to provide a visual rather than a written synthesis of what modern archeology has to say about the surviving traces of the early Christian Church in Rome. He wanted to create a real pictorial history of this early community, for of all the cities in the early Christian world it was probably Rome that left the largest number of historic remains in its cemeteries and churches and, above all, in the catacombs. Alas, that underground realm of death seems no longer to arouse the interest of a wide audience, now that scholars have robbed it of its former source of fascination, its supposed role as asylum and house of prayer for persecuted Christians.

But science, today, can offer us instead images of a community of the faithful, with their daily ups and downs, the great events of their history, their worries and hopes and,

2. Mother and Child, detail of the lunette with praying figure, chamber of the veiled woman. Catacomb of Priscilla.

3. Row of "tabernae" on the road through the Trajan marketplace gives an idea of city life. The Christians were undoubtedly a part of it.

4. Hypothetical reconstruction of the "domus ecclesia" beneath the basilica of Saints John and Paul. It was a two-story dwelling in whose right wing – marked in red – a large hall was built for the cult during the fourth century (from Frankl).

5. Praying figure. This was part of the fourth century fresco decoration of the ground floor of the "domus ecclesia".

4

above all, their religious sentiments, which are at least as fascinating in their own way. This community was an ancient one, directly connected with the first years of Christian preaching, and when St. Paul reached Rome in about AD 61 he found it already well-organized and efficient. The Christians had been informed of his arrival beforehand: immediately, they arranged for groups of representatives to welcome him with the honor and exultation befitting the great apostle, although he came in chains with other prisoners – perhaps common criminals – and an escort of soldiers.

Groups of Christians hastened to the station on the Appian Way called *Tres Tabernae*, fifty kilometres from the city, and some went even farther, to the *Forum Apii*. The book of The Acts of the Apostles (28, 14-15) says that St. Paul was moved and drew courage from this fact, and was persuaded thereby that the Christian message had already grown deep roots in Rome.

And indeed, these roots continued to grow and gain strength. In vain did Nero's persecution eliminate a "vast multitude" of believers (to use the expression of the pagan, Tacitus); in vain did tempests and disturbances strike again and again during the next two centuries: they caused the community trouble and pain, but they never shook its solid foundations.

The constant growth of the community forced its leaders to adopt more rational forms of organization, a step in keeping with the Roman spirit especially during a period when all the civilized world was governed from the city, and the Church was soon subdivided into groups – perhaps on the model of the enormous Jewish colony that already existed in Rome. In fact, the early Roman Christians retained a memory of their Jewish origins for quite a long time.

As late as the fifth century, the two traditions were represented in basilica mosaics (in Santa Pudenziana (109) and Santa Sabina, for example) by the symbolic figures of the *ecclesia ex circumcisione* and the *ecclesia ex gentibus.* It is almost certain that no specific preacher brought the Gospel message to Rome, as was the case in many churches elsewhere – St. Paul would have mentioned it, especially if the evangelist had been St. Peter. Rather, Christianity seems to have sprung up spontaneously in the heart of the Roman Jewish community, which was largely composed of tradespeople whose contact with their homeland must have brought them early knowledge of the impact produced by the preaching of Jesus of Nazareth and his followers. The book of The Acts of the Apostles mentions that there were "strangers of Rome" among those present on the first occasion the Apostles spoke in Jerusalem. It was almost certainly the ferment among the Jews of Rome, caused by conversions to the new doctrine, that set off the controversy and public unrest whose intensity finally led the Emperor Claudius to expel all Jews from the city in about AD 50. This is reported by the pagan writer, Suetonius, and the same story is told by St. Paul, who met exiles from the capital in Greece. But after the death of Claudius, when the exiles returned, they were already divided into two different religious beliefs and organizations.

The Christian community had by now opened its doors to converts from paganism, and had prospered thereby, for new adherents came in a continuous stream from every strata of society. But this welcoming of the pagans collided with the rigidly exclusive tradition of the Judaic communities, even those of the Diaspora, and was almost certainly what caused the final separation of Christians from Jews, a development which took place in

6

other cities as well.

The Christians of Rome were for the most part poor and humble folk. They generally lived in densely populated neighborhoods in the suburbs, especially near the sites which offered the possibility of a lively trade in supplies for the capital, or along the banks of the Tiber, or near industries like the transport services on the Appian Way. The army had shown itself from the start a favourable ground for the propagation of Christian ideas, and there were also many Christians among the workers in the field of entertainment – in the circuses, amphiteatres, theatres, and *naumachias* dedicated to the public spectacles which were so essential a part of Roman life. Many more were to be found among the masses of slaves – from the imperial palace and the rich patrician residences to the city at large, where they made up the swarms of public servants employed in construction work, in the maintenance of aqueducts, road and drainage systems, and in fire-fighting and street cleaning.

But there were also rich and powerful figures among the Christians of Rome. By the end of the first century even the niece of the Emperor Domitian, Flavia Domitilla, had been sentenced to exile as a Christian and had ended her life on the island of Ponza with a "*longum martyrium*", as St. Jerome says. Indeed, who but the wealthy could provide the economic means for organizing the Christian community? Believers gathered in their homes for the performance of eucharistic and baptismal rites, to receive religious instruction, and to assist the needy. During the third century a certain number of these rich homes became established centers of Christianity, much like modern parishes today.

In the fourth century, there were twenty-five of them. Each of these "*tituli*", as they were called, bore the name of the owner, whom the

6. Portrait of a couple with saints, painted glass. Florence, Museo Nazionale del Bargello.

7

civil authorities held juridically responsible for the property and all that went on in it. The gratitude of the Roman community was reflected in a long-cherished memory of these former benefactors, and when majestic churches later replaced the houses during the Reign of Peace, the original name was kept in nearly all of them. Throughout the fifth century, many of their former owners were even held to be saints by the populace, or were confused with martyrs bearing the same name: Sabina, Balbina, Cecilia, Anastasia, Grisogonus, Eusebius, Pudens. Archaeological excavations have only rarely revealed traces of these early household churches, and those which have been discovered lack any very evident signs of Christianity, like the *orant* (a figure with arms outstretched in prayer symbolizing the faithful) painted in a hall of

the house discovered beneath the *titulus* of Bizans del Cello. Many factors contribute to explain this. The new church was not always built precisely on the site of the old *titulus*, but frequently on more suitable neighboring ground. Or the ancient parish center might have been located in an upper-story apartment, as still happens today in many of the city's suburbs.

It is a well-known fact that the enormous population of the capital led residential Roman architecture to develop upwards, so that buildings in Rome, unlike the type of structure found in Pompeii and other cities, were up to four or five stories high. Obviously, the construction of titular basilicas towards the end of the fourth and during the fifth centuries resulted in the complete eradication of the memory of these ancient places of worship.

But the underground cemeteries still bear well-preserved traces of another aspect of the beneficence of wealthy Roman Christians towards their community: the donation of land for private burial grounds.

7. Fisherman with fishing lines, detail of the Nereidi sarcophagus. Catacomb of Protestato.

8

9

8. Banquet illustrated in a chamber of the catacomb of St. Callixtus. This ancient agape funeral rite, formerly held to be a representation of the Eucharist, is a pagan ceremonial which symbolizes loving union with the dead. The Church treated this as a rite of love and charity and tolerated it until the fifth century.

9. Fossor, or gravedigger, at work, depicted in a painting from the Catacomb of Saints Marcellinus and Peter. The overwhelmingly vast necropoli of underground Rome are the creation of these humble workers, who opened galleries and cubicula, decorated them with frescoes and then buried the dead in them.

10. Bone doll, with articulated arms and legs, found in the lime used to seal a small loculus in the cemetery of Novatian. The children's tombs in the catacombs are often furnished with a profusion of decorative objects: lamps, vessels for perfumes, toys, bells, and other mementoes of those young creatures.

The names of these cemeteries, like those of the urban *tituli*, reveal the generosity of the owners of the property in which they lie: Priscilla, Domitilla, Maximus, Thraso, Commodilla, Agnes, Ottavilla, etc. And in some of the catacombs of the pre-Constantinian period it is possible to distinguish original nuclei which were enlarged later to make room for many more graves than were necessary for the members of a single family. We have proof of Church possession, from the start, for one catacomb only, "the cemetery", as the author of the early third century *Philosophumena* calls it, where nearly all the popes of that century were buried. Its name today is St. Callixtus.

Perhaps there were other community areas as well, like the Domitilla nucleus, named after the Flavii Aurelii, but probably these, too, had their first origins in the beneficence of the wealthy, who granted the Church use of their lands as burial ground. With the passage of time, nearly all cemeteries became the property of the Church and were directly administered by it. But numerous exceptions still existed during the Reign of Peace: private cemeteries belonging to Christian families who preferred not to join the Church's funeral organization. An example was discovered on the Via Latina in 1956, a small *hypogeum* full of stupendous paintings – a regular fourth century pinacoteca!

11

The early beginnings of ecclesiastical organization date back to the time of Pope Fabian (236-50). He divided the city into seven districts and entrusted seven deacons with the supervision of the cultural, instructional and charitable activities that went on in the *tituli* of each. Another of their tasks was funeral organization, for which the state did not provide at that time, and each district was allotted a burial zone outside the walls, with a certain number of cemeteries. The plan in this volume shows their probable division. Cemeteries were not built underground out of a desire for safety from persecution, which is a romantic fantasy encouraged by the famous novels of the XIX century and still dear to the popular imagination today.

The ancients willingly made use of underground land when it could be easily and safely excavated: from time immemorial the soft tufa of Latium had favored the development of a vast network of subterranean tunnels for waterworks, of chambers and galleries for graves, and even of recreation areas concealed in places called "cryptoporticus" beneath summer villas. The Christians and Jews of Rome simply found in the underground cemetery the solution to a problem which the large number of

community members, and the choice of burial rather than cremation, had made increasingly difficult in a city where space was at a premium and suburban land was costly. The multi-levelled network of catacomb galleries could be brought to a height of five meters with further digging, and offered room for thousands of tombs along the walls and in the ground. The simplest were the *loculi*, rectangular cavities dug one above the other in the tufa walls. Each corpse was wrapped in a sheet before being placed in the tomb, which often contained two or more members of the same family. The name of the deceased was painted or sculpted on the brick or marble slab serving as its door, together with other pertinent information, usually the day and month of death. Small terracotta lamps and vases for perfume were often placed above the tomb, like the lights and flowers in cemeteries today. The sombre galleries lit by the dancing lamp flames must have made an impressive sight. A richer type of tomb was the *arcosolium*, a cell for the dead hollowed out of the tufa and often plastered and frescoed, with a horizontal slab for a lid over the grave surmounted by an arch. *Arcosolia* are most often found in *cubicula*, small rooms constituting family or corporation vaults. They are sometimes illuminated by pit-like openings in the vaulting resembling a skylight, which originally served for the removal of earth during the excavations. The catacombs were used as cemeteries until the early fifth century. The colossal development of some of them was due to the

11. Epigraph with symbols from the Pio Christian Museum. The ship guided by the lighthouse beam on its journey towards the port symbolizes the journey towards salvation with faith as the guide.

12

13

cult of the martyrs, which led the faithful to seek burial closer to the sacred tombs as a near guarantee of salvation.

When burials there came to an end, the catacombs became sanctuaries. Immense numbers of pilgrims thronged to Rome, the Holy City, from every part of Europe. In spite of the wars against the Goths in the sixth century, the Longobard raids of the seventh and the growing insecurity and poverty of the Roman countryside, the martyrs' sanctuaries were still regularly restored and embellished by the popes.

The *Itinerari*, guides for pilgrims written in the seventh and eighth centuries, show that devotion to them was still alive at that period. Nearly all of them were restored again in Pope Hadrian's time (772-95).

But during the first decades of the ninth century, relics were transferred with even greater frequency from the original tombs to churches within the city walls.

Each and every catacomb was thereby doomed to extinction, for the cult of the martyrs was the sole reason for continuing visits and regular restoration.

The entrances to that underground world finally vanished beneath subsidences of the earth and an overgrowth of vegetation, and except for a few galleries, the catacombs

remained unknown until the sixteenth century, when Antonio Bosio, "the Columbus of subterranean Rome" (1575-1629), began a systematic investigation. He located about thirty catacombs, and after him the number of new discoveries slowly grew. Unfortunately, the pillage of marble and precious objects grew as well.

But with the founding of the *Pontificia Commissione di Archeologia Sacra* in 1852, and De Rossi's extensive research which outlined a path for further study, the catacombs assumed their rightful place as the most stirring and popular of the monuments of Christian antiquity.

The most important of the Roman catacombs are illustrated in this volume with a well-paced and precise text by Fabrizio Mancinelli, who provides notes on the collection prepared by Professor Josi and shown here in Mauro Sarri's splendid photographs, taken for the Istituto Fotografico Editoriale Scala of Florence. He also provides brief additional comments to introduce the principal buildings of the cult – those which, during the Reign of Peace, lent to the capital of the Empire its new face as capital of the Christian world.

Rome, March 8, 1980

12. Firmia Victora's inscription. Pio Christian Museum.

13. Epitaph of Severa from the catacomb of Priscilla, now in the Vatican Museum. The inscription wishes the deceased a life in God, and she appears dressed in the pallium signifying nobility. The Adoration of the Magi expresses her Christian faith.

14

15

14. Sarcophagus from the Vatican cemetery, fourth century. At the center, the Law being delivered to St. Peter, who symbolizes the authority of Christ the Lawgiver. Opposite Peter is Paul, shown in a gesture of approval and acclamation. At the far sides, two scenes in evident symbolic connection: the sacrifice of Isaac, and the beginning of Christ's ordeal before the tribunal of Pilate.

15. Sarcophagus of Domitilla, now in the Vatican. Mid-fourth-century. Here we see the symbolism in artists' representations of the Passion at that time. At the center is the cross with the monogram of Christ and the crown of victory. To the right, Christ before Pilate; to the left, the Cyrenian and the coronation — but with laurel, not thorns.

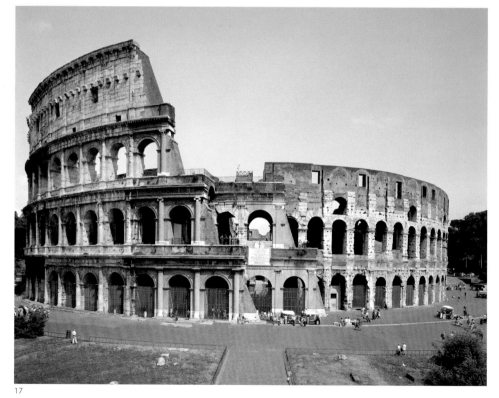

16

17

16-18. The Flavian amphiteatre, one of the most prestigious places of entertainment ever built. The Roman passion for "ludi", or games held in circus and amphiteatre, was truly incredible. After the famous fire of 64, Nero's repression of Christianity took the form of cruel spectacles given in the Circus of Caligula in the Vatican. Even in the persecutions that followed, martyrs frequently performed their sacrifice in places of entertainment – more often in the Circus Maximus than in the Colosseum. For example, we know that when crucifixions took place, the crosses were often planted along the spine, a long wall of earth which divided the arena at the center.

19

ST. JOHN LATERAN

The basilica of St. John Lateran was the first large Christian place of worship to be built within the city walls. Constantine, the emperor whose Edict of 313 granted the Christians freedom of worship, chose to erect the basilica on this site near the Laterani family residence, first of all

19. Boniface VIII opens the first Jubilee from the Benediction portico of the Lateran Palace. Milan, Biblioteca Ambrosiana.

because it belonged to him – in fact, the *equites singulares*, private guard of the Emperor, had their barracks there –, and secondly because its distance from the Forum would be less likely to irritate non-Christians. The basilica, which rises on the ruins of earlier structures, including the barracks of the *equites singulares*, was begun between 313 and 314 under the pontificate of either Pope Melchiades (311-14) or Pope Sylvester (314-35) and was dedicated to the Savior. The dedication to John the baptist and St. John the Evangelist was a later addition by Gregory the Great (590-604). In the north-northeast area to the right of

20

the basilica stood the patriarchate, residence of the pope as Bishop of Rome. The baptistery was built behind the apse, to the north west. It was the only one in existence in Constantine's time, and once a year, at Easter, the pope administered baptism there. The basilica's appearance today differs from its early Christian form, although Borromini's baroque restructuring of the naves between 1646 and 1650, commissioned by Innocent X, substantially reflects the proportions and distribution of light and space in the Constantinian basilica. The old edifice, like the present one, was built on a basilical plan with five aisles, and was 53.73 meters wide and about 30 meters high. The width of the central nave was 18.73 meters and its length 90.55 meters. It ended in a 9.22 meters deep semicircular apse pierced by ample windows, and was separated from the side aisles by a row of nineteen red granite columns with beams above. It had a trussbeam roof, perhaps left visible. Light filtered through a series of rectangular arch centred

windows. The inner aisles – 7.94 meters wide and 90.23 meters long – were lower, and took their lighting from a series of crescent windows; a row of twenty-one antique green marble columns set on high bases and connected by arches divided them from the outer aisles. These were even lower and less well-lighted, and much shorter (74.88 meters), although of almost the same width (7.69 meters). They ended in two rooms, 8.93 meters by 11.45 meters, which projected slightly on the outside, and formed a sort of small nave transept. The basilica walls were probably covered with marble and decorated with paintings at window level. The floor of the central nave was antique gold marble, and the vault of the apse was covered in gold leaf. No visible traces remain of the Constantinian patriarchate. The present Lateran Palace was built in the days of Sixtus V (1585-90), as was the *Scala Santa* edifice. However, the latter includes Early Christian structures – such as the *scrinium* with a sixth- to seventh-century fresco representing St. Augustine – as well as medieval structures like the thirteenth-century chapel of the *Sancta Sanctorum*. The adjoining Leonine *Triclinium* is the architect Ferdinando Fuga's reconstruction (1743) of the dining-room of the medieval patriarchate, built and decorated

20. Filippo Gagliardi, fresco showing the interior of St. John Lateran, 1651, Church of S. Martino ai Monti. It provides a reconstruction of the original Constantinian basilica, albeit with a few inaccuracies, such as ogival windows and arches, instead of beams, connecting the columns of the central nave.

21. Baptistery of St. John Lateran. Founded with the basilica, it stands on the remains of a villa of the first century A.D., and of a later thermal structure.

22. Plan of the basilica of St. John Lateran. The structure of the present basilica is shown in black, the foundations of the Constantinian edifice are outlined in brown.

22

by Leo III (795-816). The structure of today's Baptistery, on the other hand, is still essentially Early Christian. Its original plan was certainly round. The octagonal plan of the present edifice – about 20 meters in diameter – is the result of restoration work ordered by Sixtus III (432-40). Inside, eight porphyry columns with beams above separate the central hall from the ring-shaped chamber, once covered by a barrel vault, which surrounds it. There was originally a dome over the central hall, and eight semicircular windows for illumination. The present-day *tiburio* dates from a restoration by Paul III in 1540. In front of Sixtus III's edifice was an atrium in the shape

of a forceps, now known as the chapel of either St. Secunda and St. Rufina or St. Cyprian and St. Justin, with marble and mosaic ornamentations, partly still in place. It had a beam-roofed portico supported by two porphyry columns. The chapels of St. John the Baptist and of St. John the Evangelist, standing one to the right, the other to the left of the actual entrance, were built during the papacy of St. Hilary (461-67). The vault of the latter still has the mosaic decoration of that time, with the Mystical Lamb at its center. The chapel of St. Venantius came later. It was built by Pope John IV (640-42) and decorated by Pope Theodore (642-48).

23

ST. PETER'S

The basilica of St. Peter was erected by the Emperor Constantine and Pope Sylvester to preserve the tomb of the Prince of the Apostles, over which a commemorative monument called the Trophy of Gaius had been built towards the middle of the second century. The memorial was called a "trophy" because the word reflected the Early Christian belief that the saint's martyrdom was a victory of faith over death. The site was part of a pagan necropolis located on the slopes of *Mons Vaticanus*, not far from the Circus of Gaius and Nero where, according to tradition, the apostle was martyred in AD 64. The necropolis extended along the north side of the circus, from east to west. During the first and second centuries numerous tombs were built, some of them Christian, and all with south entrances facing the circus. They belonged to the families of wealthy freedmen – the Aelii, the Aurelii, the Caetenni, the Julii, the Marcii, the Tullii, the Ulpii, and the Falerii. Some of these originally pagan structures were later decorated by Christians, for example the Mausoleum of the Julii, seen and described for the first time by the chronicler, Tiberio Alfarano, in 1574. In the center of its vault is a mosaic representing Jesus as the Sun God, and on its walls one can still make out images whose connotations are clearly Christian. From the end of the second century, the tombs continued to spread southwards until they covered the axis of the circus, which had by then fallen into disuse. The most imposing of them, was a rotunda with a forceps-shaped atrium in front, perhaps the first of its kind. It stood only a few meters to the west of the circus obelisk (removed by Sixtus V to St. Peter's Square in 1586) and was aligned with it. Consecrated under Pope Symmachus (498-515) and dedicated to St. Andrew, it was later connected with the nearby mausoleum of Honorius at the southern extremity of the transept of the Constantinian basilica. Both of these mausoleums were originally destined to be the imperial family tombs of Theodosius. The Trophy of Gaius took its name from the presbyter who mentioned it for the first time in 200. It stood in the north-western zone of the necropolis, in an open space (Camp P) measuring approximately 7 meters by 4 meters; it was surrounded by mausoleums and sepulchral ground and bounded on the west by a red plaster-covered wall. The monument, in the shape of an aedicula, was built at the same time as the red wall, and consisted of two niches excavated in the wall itself and a third, invisible, underground niche communicating with the tomb of the apostle. The two upper niches were separated by a slab, 1.80 meters wide, resting on two small columns in front. The lower one survives in today's "Niche of the Sacred Pallia", but the upper one, which had at its center a small embrasure communicating with the outside, and may have been crowned by a tympanum, has perished with time. The

23. Plan of the monuments in the Vatican. The structures existing today are shown in black, whereas the necropoli, the circus, the Constantinian basilica with the two pre-existing rotundas and the Vatican Grottoes are in color. The square on the axis of the circus indicates the original position of the obelisk, now in St. Peter's Square. Reconstruction based on earth probe samples. Dimensions of the Circus: 590 meters in length by 95 meters in width (from Magi). * Wall of the "carceres" the starting point for quadriga chariot races, now under the Palazzo delle Congregazioni Romane.

24

entire monument was approximately 2.30 meters high. During the third century, two small walls were added to the north and south of the lower niche. The north wall has graffiti with invocations to the apostle. The niche and the floor in front of it were covered with

25

marble, and the open space with a mosaic. The basilica was built between 320-21 and about 329 to create a monumental setting dedicated to the memory of the apostle, and to favor the growth of his cult among the great mass of believers. The major components of the structure must have been completed before the death of the emperor in 337. In order to create a platform for the building, the Constantinian architects had to bury the necropolis and dig out part of the hill to the north. In front of the basilica stood a large rectangular atrium with porticoes inside, on the entrance side of the church facade. In the center of the courtyard was the fountain with the bronze pine cone, now to be seen in the Vatican Palace courtyard which bears its name. It was protected by a bronze canopy supported by four porphyry columns and crowned by a variety of objects, including the two bronze peacocks currently on display in the new wing of the Vatican Museum. Inside the basilica were five aisles separated by twenty-two columns of various colors, with a beamed roof in the central nave and connecting arches in the side aisles. Like their bases and capitals these were spoil taken from more ancient buildings. The five aisles led to the transept, and then to the apse, with

24. Reconstruction of Camp P. The spot over St. Peter's tomb in the necropolis was marked by a monument, in the shape of an aedicula, located in the so-called Camp P, a cemetery zone which was bounded to the west by the "red wall" containing the monument niches. The plan of the basilica had the monument situated on the chord of the apse (from Apollony Ghetti).

25. Reconstruction of the apse of the Constantinian basilica. (from Toynbee-Ward Perkins).

26

27

26. Ivory Pola casket
with the Constantinian
arrangement of the tomb
of St. Peter (Venice,
Archaeological Museum).

27. Giovanni Battista Ricci
da Novara, Interior of the
Constantinian basilica of St.
Peter, detached fresco from
the Vatican grottos, now in
the Sacristy, sixteenth century.

28. Pine cone. Vatican, Courtyard of the cone.

29

St. Peter's funeral monument dominant at the center. A marble parallelepiped set off the second-century aedicula, visible through a double door in it on the nave side. This coffer-like structure sat upon a marble-covered platform which was raised a step higher than the transept floor. Above it was a bronze canopy supported by four twisted columns. Beam work connected them to two more twisted columns situated at the very end of the apse, which contained a vault covered with gold leaf. The Constantinian columns survive in the present basilica, beside the niches in the cupola pillars dedicated to St. Longinus, St. Andrew, St. Helen and St. Veronica. The central nave was better lit than the other aisles, thanks to eleven windows in the upper part of both its walls and a double row of windows in the facade It ended in a triumphal arch at the transept, whereas the side aisles had only two columns with beams between. The roof over the central nave was pitched to both sides and over the two side aisles towards the outer side only. The transept served as a *martyrium*. It was lower than the central nave, ending with exedrae both to the north and to the south. These were lower than the transept, and they projected beyond the walls of the nave and aisles. The basilica designed by the Constantinian architects had various functions: it was an assembly hall for the resident population, a *martyrium*, a church and object of pilgrimages, a covered cemetery and, finally, a hall for banquet and funeral libations. It had no fixed altar. The first altar dates back to the time of Gregory the Great (590-604), when the presbytery was raised, altering the Constantinian project so that Mass could be celebrated directly above the tomb of the apostle. Others sustain that some of the changes were introduced during the papacy of Pelagius II between 579 and 590. The presence of Peter's tomb was signaled, however, by the ciborium and altar, which were placed directly above the tomb. The basilica of St. Peter was larger than that of St. John. The atrium was 90.92 meters deep and its width the same as that of the church, 63.42 meters. The central nave was 90.95 meters long and 25.15 meters wide, and the side aisles had the following widths: 9.49 meters (outer south aisle), 9.78 meters (inner south aisle), 9.79 meters (inner

29. Peacock of gilded bronze. Vatican, New wing.

30. Sarcophagus of Probus, end of fourth century. St. Peter's, Grottoes. In the central niche, a beardless Christ with the jewelled cross in His right hand and a scroll in His left stands on a hill from which issue the four rivers of Paradise. Saints Peter and Paul are to the side. In the side niches are the other apostles in groups of two.

30

31

north aisle), 9.21 meters (outer north aisle). The transept measured 66.43 meters by 16.82, the exedrae 10.76 meters by 16.82. The church height at the facade was about 38.48 meters, but the transept was little more than 25 meters high. Today the only remains of the original basilica are to be found in the so-called Vatican Grottoes, which are level with the floor of the Constantinian edifice, and in the necropolis below it. Nevertheless a fairly accurate picture can be formed from various ancient illustrations. In the ivory bas-relief of the ivory Pola casket (440 ca), known also as

Samagher Box, the Constantinian disposition of the monument to the apostle appears with great clarity.

A sixteenth century fresco by Giovanni Battista Ricci da Novara also shows a vertical section of the church, with the naves ending in the so-called "dividing wall", erected in 1538 so that religious functions could go on while the new building was under construction. Finally, a drawing by Domenico Tasselli, dated about 1611, illustrates the exterior of the old basilica, with the atrium, the pinecone fountain and the façade.

31. Sarcophagus of Junius Bassus, fourth century. St. Peter's, Treasury. Above, center, the "Traditio Legis"; below, the entrance into Jerusalem. The other episodes are, above, the Sacrifice of Abraham, the Capture of St. Peter, the Capture of Christ, and Christ before Pilate; below, Job, Adam and Eve, Daniel in the Lion's Den, and St. Paul led to his martyrdom. The artist clearly intended to unite the supreme sacrifice of the fathers of the Roman Church and the Passion of Christ.

32. Mosaic with Christ as Sun God in Mausoleum M of the Julii. St. Peter's, Pre-Constantinian necropoli.

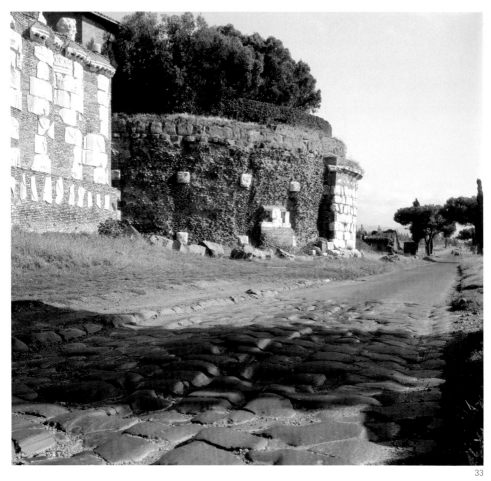

33

SAN SEBASTIANO

The church of San Sebastiano, once *basilica apostolorum,* stands on the righ-hand side of the Appian Way, about two kilometers from the Porta San Sebastiano.

On the other side of the road, slightly further south, are the Circus of Maxentius and his son, Romulus', tomb.

In ancient times this spot was a deep hollow, used as a pozzolana stone quarry and dubbed *ad catacumbus,* a term which in modern times has come to be a synonym for "underground cemetery".

The catacomb of St. Sebastian originated in the galleries of the abandoned pit probably as early as the first century, and was developed towards the north and east mainly during the third century.

The oldest building in the area was a villa constructed during the first century, to the

west of the pit. It had a nearly square plan, and the rooms were arranged on two stories around a central courtyard. The entrance faced west onto a small street, parallel to the Appian Way.

Another similar, but later, edifice found under the basilica, the so-called *Villa Piccola,* contains geometric decorations characteristic of the wall painting of the time.

Along the north wall of the first villa and beyond it, at the edge of the hollow, were a series of mausoleums also from the first century. They lined the sides of a small street in a double file.

Towards the middle of the second century, the bottom of the hollow was earthed over to create a small level open space, about 9 meters below the present church floor. On one side of it three mausoleums were built in succession.

The oldest is probably the one called the "mausoleum of the axe". Shortly before 260 – perhaps in 258 – the clearing was covered with enough earth to raise the ground level by about 6 meters.

On this new open area the *memoria* of St. Peter and St. Paul was built, bounded

33. View of the Roman pavement of the Appian Way, along which many important catacombs are found.

34. Catacomb of St. Sebastian, view of the three mausoleums.

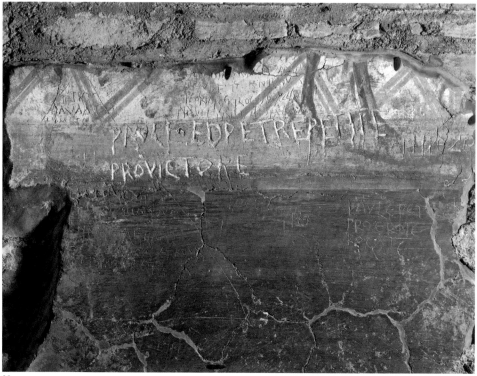

35

on the north by the row of first-century
mausoleums, and on the west by the villa.
The complex had a trapezoidal plan, and
extended 23 meters from east to west and 18
meters from north to south. It was essentially
a brick-paved courtyard with two covered
loggias all along the northern and eastern
sides. A steep stairway in the center led down
to an underground spring which supplied the
water necessary for the *refrigeria*, or funeral
libations.
The eastern loggia, known as the *triclia*,
was raised 1.15 meters above the courtyard
pavement. Its walls were painted with flowers,
birds and animals, but there is barely a trace
of them left today.
Instead, numerous graffiti have been found
with invocations to the Apostles, Peter
and Paul. The entry faced east, towards
the Appian Way, which was about sixty
meters away. In the northwest corner of
the courtyard the supposed *cella memoriea*
stood, its lower portion consisting of a small
southwards facing niche, with two terracotta
columns beside it stuccoed and painted to
look like marble.
The upper part of the monument has been

destroyed and cannot be reconstructed. In the
opposite wall of the courtyard, not far from
the southwest corner, was the so-called "S-
cell", a rectangular exedra with an apse and
two columns in front of it, successively used
as a mausoleum.
The Early Christian basilica differed
enormously from the present day church,
which acquired its new appearance during the
seventeenth century.
It was built during the first half of the fourth

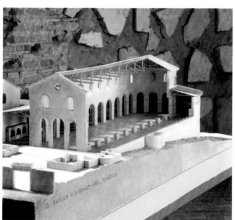

36

35. Third century graffiti
in the "triclia" beneath the
basilica, with invocations to
the apostles Peter and Paul.
Catacomb of St. Sebastian.

36. Model of the old
Early Christian basilica of
St. Sebastian (from Pacini).
The two side naves were
joined by an ambulatory.
This was a typical

architectural feature of
Constantinian temples.

37

38

37. Wall decoration of the "Villa Piccola", about 230-240. Catacomb of St. Sebastian. This is a typical example of the stylized decoration of the period, in which the architectonic elements of the Pompeian style are reduced to mere graphic notation.

38. Construction (from Tolotti) and model (from Pacini) of the memorial to St. Sebastian.

39

century on the area comprising the *memoria* and the preexisting necropolis.

Experts are not in agreement about the date of its construction, but it was built somewhere between 310 and 350. Perhaps it was begun under Maxentius.

39. Fresco with bird and fruit-bowl in the Mausoleum of Marcus Clodius Hermes. Catacomb of St. Sebastian.

If so, it would be the prototype for the Constantinian basilicas of Sant'Agnese, San Lorenzo and Santi Marcellino e Pietro. It had the same east-west axis as the *memoria* and consisted of a central nave, flanked by two small side aisles joined by an ambulatory in the apse, to the west, and at the entrance, to the east. The U-shape of the whole resembled that of a circus.

A row of pillars with connecting arches separated the central nave from the side aisles. Ample arch windows lighted the central nave, which had a trussbeam roof and was 58.30 meters long and 13.50 meters wide. The 7-meterwide side aisles and ambulatory received less light. The total length of the interior was 73.40 meters.

A crypt was built, probably during the papacy of Damasus I (366-384), with a central altar that stood on a tomb, believed to be that of St Sebastian.

At the beginning of the following century the ceiling of the crypt was removed so that the venerated tomb would be visible from the basilica. Outstanding among the numerous mausoleums lining the southern flank of the basilica and all erected in the fourth century is the rotunda of the Uranii (about 349). The Platonia mausoleum lies at the very end of the group, to the west.

Medieval tradition had it that this mausoleum was built by Pope Damasus (366-84) in honor of the Prince of the Apostles and decorated with the *platoma*, a marble slab mentioned in the *Liber pontificalis*.

40

CATACOMB OF ST. CALLIXTUS

According to the sources, the catacomb of St. Callixtus (Via Appia Antica, 102) is the oldest official cemetery of the Christian community of Rome.

The complex was named after the deacon Callixtus, who was appointed head of the cemetery under Pope Zephyrinus (199-217) and who, when he was himself pope (217-22), enlarged it greatly.

No less than nine third-century popes were buried here, in a crypt whose name reflects the fact. At certain points the cemetery complex is developed on as many as five levels, and its galleries spread over a distance of more than ten kilometres. The oldest part, situated to the right of the Appian Way as you leave Rome, presents two second-century independent galleries.

The catacomb of St. Callixtus, like the other catacombs, lay forgotten for a long while; the memory of where it stood was lost soon after the relics of the martyrs had been transferred to churches within the city and the Appia Ardeatina *memoria* removed to St. Sebastian's – the one place that people

40. Christ and the Samaritan. Catacomb of St. Callixtus.

continued to visit. The rooms of the crypts of Lucina had been known since the 18th century but it was Giovanni Battista De Rossi who discovered the burial site of pope Cornelius (251-53) in 1852, and then went on to discover the crypt of the popes in 1854 and Severus' chamber. The Crypt of the Popes (40), contains the tombs of nine Pontiffs who reigned between 230 and 283: St. Pontian (230-35), St. Anterus (236), St. Fabian (236-50), St. Lucius I (253-54), St. Stephen I (254-57), St. Sixtus II (257-58), St. Dionysius (259-68), St. Felix I (269-74) and St. Eutychian (275-83); and in 1856 he uncovered Deacon Severus' chamber. Beside the popes lie three African bishops who died during a journey to Rome: Urban, Numidian and Octatus.

At the moment the plan of the crypt is rectangular. A skylight provides illumination, and loculi and niches for sarcophagi line the side walls; it is probably an adaptment of a double chamber. However the original layout is now lost due to the final phases of the work and the significant restoration carried out during the nineteenth century by De Rossi.

On the rear wall, a marble slab reconstructed by De Rossi bears an ode written by Pope Damasus (366-84) in honor of the martyrs and bishops there laid to rest.

In the cubiculum that Deacon Severus had erected for himself and his family with the

41

permission of Pope Marcellinus (296-304), there is a marble *transenna* or screen which has an inscription containing the very first reference to the Bishop of Rome as "Pope" (298).

Opposite Deacon Severus' cubiculum is the cubiculum of the five saints, with a wall painting showing six figures in a garden full of flowers, their arms outstretched in the typical attitude of prayer. Each figure has his name inscribed at his side with the greeting, "in peace".

The painting may be dated from the beginning of the fourth century, and in it the so-called compendium technique was used for the figures, each one taking shape with only a few, essential strokes of the brush. One of the oldest nuclei of the St. Callixtus cemetery complex is the crypt of Lucina, where De Rossi found the traces which led him to discover the rest of the catacomb. Pope Cornelius lies here.

He died an exile in *Centumcellae* (Civitavecchia) in 253, and was removed to St. Callixtus' afterwards. On his tomb is the appellation, "martyr", a later addition.

The painting decorating the crypt shows the

Good Shepherd, an allusion to Christ; it is an early third century work, executed with a very rapid compendium technique. Also part of the original cemetery were the cubicula of the Sacraments, so-called because they are decorated with paintings that was thought alluding to the Baptism and the Eucharist. Among the many subjects depicted in these frescoes, which date from the first half of the third century, are the stories of Jonah, the Evangelical Fisherman, the Banquet of the Seven Disciples at Lake Tiberias, the Healing of the Paralytic, the Baptism of Jesus, Abraham's Sacrifice, and a banquet scene.

42

41, 42. Cubiculum of the Five Saints. Catacomb of St. Callixtus. In fact, in this fresco there are six praying figures. They are shown in a garden, which symbolizes the abode of eternal happiness – parddeisos is the Greek term for garden. Beside each figure is a name: Dionysia, Nemestus, Procopius, Eliodora, Zoe, Arcadia.

43

43. Eucharistic banquet in the crypt of the Sacraments. Catacomb of St. Callixtus. The scene represented in this illustration could hardly be taken for a simple pagan funeral meal. It appears in several places in the Roman catacombs; and although it varies in form, it always contains the symbolic number of baskets filled with bread, a detail which is lacking in frescoes which clearly depict a refrigerium, or funeral banquet. The baskets commemorate the miracle wrought by Jesus in the desert, when he provided bread for the famished multitude. In the Gospel according to Saint John, in the famous discourses on the bread of heaven which abideth unto eternal life, this miracle is explicitly connected with the Eucharist. The other part of that rite is represented by a catacomb painter in the near-by crypt of Lucina, where a glass of red wine has been set among the loaves in the symbolic basket.

44

44. Fish and eucharistic bread. Catacomb of St. Callixtus.

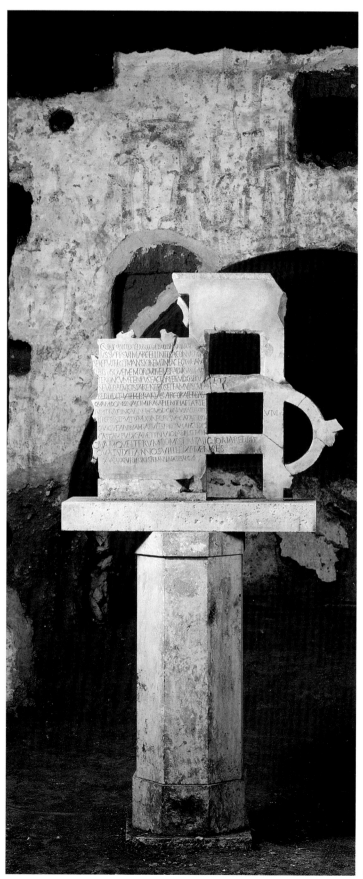

46. Epitaph of Deacon Severus, Catacomb of St. Callixtus. Here it is stated that this cleric, with the authorization of Pope Marcellinus (296-304), had a double cubiculum with an arcosolium and a skylight built to serve as tomb for himself and his family. The inscription also alludes to the resurrection of the dead: Young Severa will lie in this house of peace until the Lord restores to her body its immortal soul.

47. Christ and the Samaritan. Catacomb of St. Callixtus.

48. Plan of the catacomb of Domitilla showing only the zone near the basilica of Saints Nereus and Achilleus. The different colors indicate the different catacomb levels. The basilica is in black. The fairly chaotic appearance of tombal excavations in this area sets it apart from the rest of the catacombs, which feature a regular network of long galleries intersected at right angles by an orderly series of cubicula. Here, in the oldest part of the cemetery, the small, originally independent family nuclei were joined together only later, when the burial ground was unified under community ownership. Then its organization improved, and excavation work was entrusted to specialized gravediggers. But the crowding of subterranean dwellings at this point was also due to the desire of the faithful for burial in the vicinity of the martyrs' sanctuary. It frequently produced a dangerous weakening of the tufa layers and, as a result, archaeologists generally find the crypt of the martyrs buried under awesome landslides.

1st storey
2nd storey
Hypogeum of the Flavi
3th storey
4th storey
Buildings
Pagan Hypogeum

Via delle Sette Chiese

N

48

CATACOMB OF DOMITILLA

One of the most extensive underground cemeteries in Rome, the catacomb of Domitilla originated with the establishment of several small cemeteries on lands belonging to Flavia Domitilla and given by her to her freedmen. Its entrance lies between Piazza dei Navigators and the beginning of Via Ardeatina. Flavia Domitilla, niece of Flavius Clemens, consul in AD 95, was indirectly related to the imperial family. Her Christian faith led Domitian to exile her on the island of Ponza, where she died. The catacomb was developed mainly on two levels – only rarely is there a third or fourth story of galleries and cubicula. In the chambers known as the Hypogeum of the Flavi family, De Rossi believed he had found the tombs of the Christian members of the family of Flavia Domitilla, while it is now identified as a pagan hypogeum datable to the end of the third or early fourth century, later converted

to Christianity and enlarged during the fourth century. Towards the end of the third century the bodies of the martyrs Nereus and Achilleus were placed in a crypt on the third level. It was transformed by Pope Damasus (366-84) into a small masonry basilica, and enlarged to its present size (31 meters long and from 17 to 12 meters wide) between 390 and 395 by Pope Siricius. At the end of the fourth century, the basilica – which has now been rebuilt along the essential lines of the original – had its upper part projecting above the ground, and its floor on the level of the second story of the catacomb. A narthex stood in front of the main edifice, which had three aisles separated by two rows of four columns with connecting arches; the columns were plundered from other buildings, as were their capitals. The central nave, about 20 meters long and from 8.50 to 10 meters wide, rose above side aisles 3.50 to 4 meters in width: its illumination came from two rows of wide centered arch windows, and it ended in an apse to the west. There were probably *matronei,* or women's galleries, above the side aisles. The altar area was bounded by a series of *transennae,* and a marble ciborium set off the altar, which was placed over the martyrs' tomb. Of the ciborium, only the supporting columns

49, 50. Fresco and Cubiculum of the Good Shepherd. Catacomb of Domitilla. There are many frescoes depicting the Good Shepherd in this section of the catacomb. In some there is an orans figure behind each sheep, meaning that Christ transports another soul to the place of eternal bliss.

51

52

remain, with St. Achilleus' martyrdom depicted on one of them. The entry to the basilica of Saints Nereus and Achilleus was up a stairway leading to a side door in the narthex, just as it is today. During the eighth century, the building was stripped of everything that could be carried away, including the flooring, and afterwards the whole structure collapsed – perhaps as a result of the earthquake of 897. It was unearthed during excavations in 1873-74. In a small cubiculum, dug out right behind the apse of the basilica, is the arcosolium of the Veneranda. The fresco on the rear lunette, painted after 356, shows the deceased Veneranda being led into the garden of paradise by a young maiden, identified for a long time as St. Petronilla. This

is, however, a late and hardly credible tradition. A large staircase linking the first and second levels of the catacomb was discovered in 1854. On its wall a fresco, dating from about the middle of the third century, shows a young shepherd holding a panpipe – a primitive wind instrument – in his hand, surrounded by his flocks of sheep and rams, with four hills enclosing the scene in the background. The figure symbolizes Christ, the Good Shepherd of the parable (John 10, 1-16), as described on the cippus of Bishop Abercius now displayed in the Lateran Museum. The landscape in the illustration is evidence of this source: "The holy shepherd who leads his flocks to pasture on the mountains and in the valley".

51. Arcosolium of Veneranda. Catacomb of Domitilla

52. Catacomb of Domitilla. Christ the Teacher among the Apostles. Fresco, dated mid-fourth century. This decoration of an arcosolium in the so-called crypt of

Ampliatus shows Christ, beardless, in the role of teacher. Two of the apostle figures were unfortunately destroyed during excavation of a loculus under the fresco.

53. Veneranda and St Petronilla martyr. Catacomb of Domitilla.

54

CATACOMB OF PRISCILLA

Located at 430 Via Salaria, this two level catacomb was probably named after Priscilla of the Acilii, a senatorial family whose name appears in one of the inscriptions in the Acili hypogeum on the first level.

It differs from the other catacombs in its origins, for it grew up on the site of an *arenarium*, or pozzolana stone quarry, which had been abandoned after its entrance was blocked by a slide on the Via Salaria side. Christians began using the ample and irregular galleries on the first floor of the catacomb towards the beginning of the third century.

They built about twenty tombs and niches, and hollowed hundreds of loculi out of the walls, but most of these were later hidden by masonry added to prevent the walls caving in.

The oldest sepulchres are on this level, including the Acili hypogeum and the so-called *"Cappella greca"*, built in the advanced third century.

The chapel is a rectangular chamber divided by a large arch into two spans, the second having three great niches in its walls. It was named "Greek Chapel" from the two Greek inscriptions in the right-hand niche, with dedications by a certain Obrinus to his cousin and companion Palladius, and to his

54. Scenes from the life of a deceased woman in the chamber of the "Velatio". Catacomb of Priscilla.

wife, Nestoriana.

Against the left-hand wall is a long masonry bench. The second century decoration consists of ornamental frescoes and biblical subjects covering the ceiling vault and the upper part of the walls, and stucco panels with marbled painting below.

On the arch in the first span is the Adoration of the Magi (Matthew, 2), symbol of the foundation of the church. The oldest of all known illustrations of the Virgin with Child appears there as well. On the entrance wall are the three Hebrews in the Fiery Furnace (Daniel 3, 15-24; 43-50), the symbol of faith, and Moses bringing forth water from the rock (Exodus, 17, 6), a prefiguration of the Baptism.

On the side walls are the Healing of the Sick of the Palsy (Matthew 9, 2; Mark 2, 2; Luke 5, 18), a symbol of penitence, and the stories of Susanna (Daniel, 13), which symbolize faith in God in the face of persecution and affliction: the perfidious elders are shown on the left attempting to ensnare the unfortunate Susanna, while on the right Susanna and Daniel offer up their thanks to God.

Further on, next to the entrance wall, is the phoenix dying in the flames, symbol of the resurrection of the body.

Above the apse niche is a funerary banquet; sitting at the table are seven persons, among them a woman with veiled head.

At the far left, a bearded figure, dressed in tunic and pallium, extends his arm to break the bread.

On the table before him are a chalice of wine, a plate with two fishes, and one with

55

five loaves of bread. The composition is bordered by seven baskets of bread, three to one side, four to the other. The chapel faces onto the so-called *Cryptoporticus* or underground portico, a vast area with a rectangular plan and a cross-vault ceiling in masonry, like the walls.

Another interesting burial chamber, built after the chapel, is the cubiculum of the Velatio, decorated with paintings from the second half of the third century. Its name comes from a fresco on the back wall showing scenes from the life of the deceased, who appears at the center with her arms raised in an attitude of prayer. (At her feet is the signature of an illustrious later visitor, Antonio Bosio (1575-1629), who discovered the Roman catacombs and published the first scientific studies of them).

On the left a bishop gives his blessing at the dead women's wedding, while the youth at her side hands her the nuptial veil (*flammeum*); the scroll in the bride's hands is the *tabula nuptialis*, a document enumerating marital duties.

The woman as mother is shown on the right with a baby in her arms, a group which was thought in the past to represent the Madonna and Child.

On the wall to the left of the *Velatio* fresco is the Sacrifice of Abraham (Genesis 22,

9-10), and on the wall to the right are the three Hebrews in the Fiery Furnace (Daniel 3, 19-26), another most interesting iconographical representation; in it a dove appears with a branch in its beak as symbol of divine intervention.

The vault has a painting of the Good Shepherd at the center and a cycle of stories of Jonah (Jonah 1, 1-15).

Many popes were buried on the first level of the catacomb: Sylvester (314-35) who lies in the small *ad corpus* basilica he had built over the tomb of St. Felix and St. Philip; Liberius (352-56), Siricius (384-99), Celestine I (422-32) and Vigilius (537-55) as well.

The second level is quite different in character, for its galleries, unlike the casually winding passageways of the first, were designed in accordance with a precise plan: it has two long parallel galleries with ramifications in a fishbone pattern, and the original entrance was above ground through two large stairways.

The four underground connections between the galleries of the two stories are later additions.

Many saints also rest in this catacomb. Guides for pilgrims of the High Middle Ages mention other saints that were believed to be buried here, such as Pudenziana, Prassede and Prisca.

55. The three children in the fiery furnace in the chamber of the "Velatio". Catacomb of Priscilla.

56. The Virgin and Child with the prophet Balaam. It is one of the earliest depictions of the Virgin and is to be found in the vault of one of the galleries of the arenarium. Catacomb of Priscilla.

57. The "Cappella Greca", or cubiculum of the "Fractio panic". Catacomb of Priscilla.

58

58. Bust of Christ, late fourth-early fifth century. Catacomb of Commodilla, cubiculum of an employee of the "annona" – the revenue and food supplies administration –, whose name was Leo. This is among the first of the bearded images of Christ.

59. Madonna enthroned with Child and with Saints Felix and Adauctus. Catacomb of Commodilla.

CATACOMB OF COMMODILLA

Rediscovered in 1903 by the *Pontificia Commissione di Archeologia Sacra* (Papal Commission of Sacred Archeology) – it had first been sighted in 1720 – this catacomb is located at 42 Via delle Sette Chiese and takes its name from the owner of the land, the matron Commodilla. The martyrs Felix and Adauctus, Merita and Nemesius are buried here. Felix was a priest. He was being led to the place appointed for his death when Adauctus, a stranger, came to meet him, and declared himself a Christian. For this, he was put to death with the priest. The crypt of these martyrs, at the foot of the original entrance stairway, was built during the Pontificate of Siricius (384-99), who enlarged a pre-existing sacellum. It has an irregular plan, with two arcosolia and two apses, one of them on the right. The wall frescoes were painted at various periods. To the left of the entrance, above the tomb of St. Nemesius, is the image of the second half of the VII century of a *traditio clavium*: at the center a beardless Christ, sitting on a globe, holds out the keys to St. Peter, whose hands are veiled; on the right, St. Paul holds the scrolls of the law in similarly veiled hands; to the sides are the saints Felix, Stephen and Merita. At the rear of the crypt, to the left, is a large sixth-

century fresco showing the Madonna and Child seated on a richly ornamented throne; to her left are Saints Felix and Adauctus, who are introducing a deceased woman named *Turtura* – a "turtle-dove" as the inscription below says, both in name and in deed.

59

60. The basilica of Saint Felix and Saint Adauctus. Catacomb of Commodilla. The two martyrs are portrayed on the central tomb, and they appear six times more in frescoes decorating other parts of the catacomb. Saint Luke, the evangelist, is painted on the pillar to the right, with a surgical instruments bag, the first time that the saint is portrayed with doctor's insignia. The fresco dates from the reign of the Byzantine Emperor Constantine IV (668-685).

61. Jesus predicts the denial of Peter, mid 4th century. Catacombs of Commodilla.

CATACOMB OF PRAETEXTATUS

Situated at 11 Via Appia Pignatelli, this catacomb was named after the original owner of the land, who may have been a member of the Cecili family, or maybe named after a pre-existent toponym. It dates as far back as the second century, and originated in a pagan outdoor cemetery, not far from the villa of Herodes Atticus, tutor of the sons of Marcus Aurelius. St. Januarius was buried here, as were Saints Felicissimus and Agapitus, and

62. Winter, represented in the Crypt of the Seasons. Catacomb of Praetextatus. The fresco, dated fourth century, decorated the ceiling vault of the crypt of St. Januarius, located in the Spelunca Magna, where four overlying tiers are painted with figures alluding to the seasons: flowers for spring, wheat for summer, grapes for autumn and the olive harvest for winter.

62

the martyrs Valerian, Tiburtius, Maximus and Quirinus.

The catacomb is composed of several originally separate nuclei, including the so-called *Scala maggiore* area – perhaps the oldest of all (beginning of the III century), decorated with frescoes of the life of Christ – and the *Spelunca magna* (beginning of the III century), a large gallery whose chambers have masonry entrances.

Above the catacomb there are two museums containing pagan and Christian sculptures.

63. Christ and the Samaritan woman, in the cubiculum of the Scala Maggiore. Catacomb of Praetextatus. The fresco, dated beginning of the third century, is part of the Christological cycle decorating the walls of the cubiculum at the foot of the stairway. The surviving episodes are the Healing of the woman who had an issue of blood for twelve years, the Resurrection of Lazarus, and another scene which has had a variety of interpretations.

CATACOMB OF VIA LATINA

This catacomb was discovered accidentally in 1955, during construction work in Via Dino Compagni. Father Antonio Ferrua, S.J. directed the excavations and had the findings published. The present entrance is a simple trap-door in the sidewalk near 258 Via Latina. The catacomb was not meant for the Christian community. It was built for a limited number of families – at least the four who seem to have commissioned the paintings decorating the chambers, and perhaps one or two more.

The paintings were done at different times within a relatively brief period, placed by Father Ferrua between 320 and 350, whereas the initial construction of the catacomb is dated about 315. These dates were based on four factors: classification of the architectonic elements; discovery of two Constantinian monograms; the presence of many pagan themes; and the character of the epigraphs. There are twelve frescoed chambers in this catacomb, each conventionally designated by a letter of the alphabet. According to Father Ferrua, the paintings may be divided into four groups, with all the frescoes in a given cubiculum

64. Chamber with the Resurrection of Lazarus. Catacomb of Via Latina.

belonging to the same group: the first group is in cubiculum A, the second in cubicula B and C, the third in chambers D, E and F, and the fourth in the six cubicula lettered from H to O (according to the Italian alphabet, which has neither J nor K).

The wealth of new elements contained in the iconography of these paintings is extraordinary, and the scenes are often modelled on prototypes heretofore unknown. Cubiculum B contains illustrations of a large number of Old Testament episodes.

In the vault of the left-hand arcosolium is a fresco with Adam and Eve, each with his hand pressed against his face in a gesture of suffering and despair; approaching them are Abel, with a lamb, and Cain, with a sheaf of wheat (Genesis 4, 3-4).

The destruction of Sodom (Genesis 19, 15-26) appears in the same vault. Lot, in flight, is old and bearded, wearing a tunic and toga, and holding his two daughters, clothed in dalmatics, by the hand.

To the right is the fire-swept city and, before it, Lot's wife, transformed into a pillar of salt. On the lunette at the back of the arcosolium is another fresco showing the seventy Jews sent for by Joseph as they enter Egypt (Genesis 46, 5-27).

Seven persons on three carts to the left represent the seventy; in the cart at the center is Jacob, with two sons, one on each side.

An Egyptian city lies to the right and the

65

Nile, runs below. In the vault of the right-hand arcosolium of the same cubiculum is Jacob's Dream (Genesis 28, 10-13). This episode, and all the others in cubiculum B are completely new to catacomb painting. Only the Cain and Abel episode appears in some sarcophagus decoration as well.

In the left-hand niche of cubiculum C, on the right, a fresco with the Sacrifice of Isaac (Genesis 22, 1-14) shows the voice of God stopping the hand of Abraham, armed with a knife and raised against his son. Below, the servant, next to the ass, awaits his master's return; this is the first time that this detail appears in catacomb painting.

The Resurrection of Lazarus (John 11) decorates the lunette and part of the left niche of the same cubiculum. A beardless Jesus, rod in hand, is surrounded by a crowd of at least eighty people.

Lazarus' tomb is a sort of *in antis* temple, with a long flight of stairs before it. Above is Moses receiving the Law (Exodus 24, 12-18) and to the right, the pillar of fire (Exodus 13, 21-22); these two episodes also appear for the first time in this catacomb. During the Middle Ages it was common practice to combine Old and New Testament episodes. In the rear lunette of the right hand

arcosolium in cubiculum F is a fresco representing Balaam. This episode too is drawn from the Old Testament (Numbers 22, 21-23) and shows Balaam astride an ass on the left and, to the right, a bearded angel brandishing a short sword. In the center a tree stands between the two figures. In the lunette of the arcosolium at the back of the cubiculum is another episode without its like in cemetery painting: Samson Smiting the Philistines (Judges 15, 14-16).

Samson can be recognized by the ass's jawbone in his right hand; on the left are the terrorstricken Philistines in flight and, on the right, the temple where the hero met

66

65. Lot in flight from Sodom. Catacomb of Via Latina, Cubiculum B.

66. Gravedigger at work. Catacomb of Via Latina.

67

68

his death. The New Testament episode of Jesus and the Samaritan woman at the well (John 4, 5-8), in the lunette of the left-hand arcosolium seems almost to parallel the Balaam episode facing it. Jesus, youthful and beardless, is clothed in a tunic and pallium, while the woman is wearing a shorter tunic, with closed shoes and earrings.
An alleged "Anatomy Lesson" (of "Philosophy Lesson") is depicted on the

67. Jacob arrives in Egypt. Catacomb of Via Latina, Cubiculum B.

68. Jesus resurrects Lazarus. Catacomb of Via Latina, Cubiculum C.

69. The sacrifice of Isaac. Catacomb of Via Latina, Cubiculum C.

70

71

lunette at the back of the right-hand arcosolium of chamber I, a large hexagonal room with a sexpartite vault ceiling.
In this scene, a group of people of varying ages, wearing the tunic and pallium, are seated on a cloth-covered bench with, in front of them, a completely naked man stretched out upon the ground. At the center of the group, an aged and bearded gentleman, clothed in the style of the Cynics

70. Balaam stopped by the angel. Catacomb of Via Latina, Cubiculum F.

71. Samson smiting the Philistines with an ass's jawbone. Catacomb of Via Latina, Cubiculum F. There were two other biblical scenes with the story of Samson in this catacomb. The painters may have wanted to establish a biblical counterpart to Hercules, the pagan God of strength.

72

73

– in only a pallium – turns towards the left, and with gesture of his right hand directs the attention of the group to the area below. A man on his left reaches out to touch the stomach of the naked man.

This scene has provoked much discussion. Some see in it a resuscitation or a miraculous healing, others, God surrounded by the Angels in the act of creating man. A third group claims that it is Aristotle and

72. Jesus and the Samaritan woman at the well. Catacomb of Via Latina, Cubiculum F. This scene may also be interpreted as the

appearance of the Angel of God to Hagar, the handmaiden of Abraham, at the well in the wilderness where she wandered.

73. Anatomy Lesson. Catacomb of Via Latina, Chamber I. This interpretation of the scene is supported by the presence in the vault of frescoes

showing individuals whose dedication to a life of study is indicated by a codex or scroll in their hand or by their dress.

his disciples, and a fourth, which includes Father Ferrua, holds that it is a scene from everyday life alluding to the profession of the deceased man buried in the sarcophagus below. According to the last interpretation, it is a lesson in anatomy, and the deceased is the central figure wearing only the pallium and surrounded by his colleagues and disciples.

Cubiculum N is a large square chamber with a cross-vault ceiling.

At the corners, four tufa columns with ionic-style marble bases and capitals support four triangular pediments resting on three large corbels.

The side walls are taken up by two deep arcosolia and the rear wall gives onto cubiculum O.

Unlike the latter, which is frescoed with stories from the Old and New Testament, chamber N is dedicated entirely to the myth of Hercules, here again the Christian repertory alternates with pagan themes.

The two most important episodes appear in the lunettes at the back of the arcosolia: in the one to the left, Alcestis offers to sacrifice her life for that of the dying Admetus while, in the one to the right, Hercules leads Alcestis back from Hades. Behind the hero is Cerberus, guardian of the pit, and on his right Admetus waiting, lance in hand, in a house with raised curtains. On a wall inside the right hand arcosolium is Hercules in the garden of the Hesperides.

In this portrait, unlike the others, the hero is shown as a beardless youth.

His club is leaning up against a rock and his left shoulder is covered by a Nemean lion skin.

On the left is a serpent – perhaps an allusion to original sin – winding its body round the forbidden tree, instead of the dragon of the legend. But in the legend it was in fact Atlas, not Hercules, who stole the golden apples from the garden of the Hesperides.

On the opposite wall of the same arcosolium, Hercules kills the Hydra. Here the hero is naked, bearded, and less youthful than in the garden of the Hesperides.

The other episodes depicted on the walls of this cell are Hercules and Athena clasping hands, and Hercules killing an enemy.

On the vault garlands of wheat set off the ribs and form rounds inside which cupids harvest and reap the crop.

74

75

74. Hercules killing the Hydra. Catacomb of Via Latina, Cubiculum N

75. Hercules in the garden of the Hesperides. Catacomb of Via Latina, Cubiculum N.

76

76. View of the right-
hand arcosolium of
Cubiculum N. Catacomb
of Via Latina. Notice the
elegant architecture of this
chamber. In the lunette,

Hercules is shown bringing
the heroic Alcestis back
from Hades to her husband
Admetus, for whom she
had sacrificed her life.
The legendary scene,

symbol of conjugal love,
might also serve to instruct
Christians, just as other
pagan myths most certainly
did – the story of Cupid
and Psyche, for example,

and the figure of Orpheus,
the musician.

78

CATACOMB OF SAINTS MARCELLINUS AND PETER

The site of this catacomb at 641 Via Casilina – formerly Via Labicana – was once called *ad dual lauros,* which indicated not only the cemetery area, but a vast estate of the emperor including the catacomb and bounded by Porta Maggiore, Via Labicana, Via Prenestina and Centocelle. Another name for the area was ad. S. *Helenam*, because the mausoleum of St. Helen once stood here, whose ruins alone survive today. On this spot, where the *Equites Singulares Augusti,* guard of the Emperor, had had their necropolis from the second century on, a Christian catacomb arose during the latter part of the third century. It provided a final resting place for the bodies of the numerous Christians martyred during Diocletian's persecution. First of all there were Saints Marcellinus and Peter, who gave the catacomb its name, then St. Tiburtius, St. Gorgonius, and the Four Crowned Saints, and finally the forty unknown martyrs. In the course of the fourth century, the martyrs' crypts were enlarged and embellished, and Pope Damasus (366-84) created a special

monumental setting for the crypts of Tiburtius and Gorgonius, and for Marcellinus and Peter. There were further transformations and embellishments in the fifth century, and in the sixth as well, up to the Pontificate of Honorius I (625-38). The monumental complex which stood above the subterranean necropolis was Constantinian, and was built by order of the emperor. It consisted of a large cemeterial basilica ending in a portico, with a narthex in front connected to the mausoleum that Constantine had built for his burial. A sarcophagus had even been made, but the emperor moved to Byzantium, leaving both tomb and mausoleum empty. They were later used for St. Helen, mother of Constantine. The sarcophagus, in dark red Egyptian porphyry, has on all four sides high-relief decorations representing victorious Romans and Barbarian prisoners. In 1153-54 it was transferred to St. John Lateran and reused by Pope Anastasius IV, but Pope Pius VI had it removed to the Vatican in 1778, and it is displayed there today in the Pio Clementine Museum. The basilica complex as a whole was perfectly well-known in the sixteenth-century, and in 1594 the first accurate description of

77. Summer. Catacomb of Saints Marcellinus and Peter.

78. Reconstruction of the basilica of Saints Marcellinus and Peter, with two colonnades at the sides and in front a narthex communicating with the

mausoleum of St. Helen (from Guyon).

79

the monument appeared, by Antonio Bosio. There have been several excavations between the end of the last century and present times – Henry J. Stevenson's between 1896 and 1898, Friedrich W. Deichmann's in 1940 and 1954-58, and those of the Ecole of Rome in 1975. These have made it possible to acquire a fairly precise idea of its original appearance. The basilica's functions, plans and dimensions were analogous to those of other Roman cemetery buildings of the period: the *Memoria apostolorum* – now San Sebastiano – on the Via Appia, San Lorenzo on the Tiburtina, and Sant'Agnese on the Nomeriana. Its plan was in the form of a circus, with two side aisles

79. Sarcophagus of St. Helen, kept in the Greek-cross-shaped hall in the Pio Clementine Museum in the Vatican.

making a continuous deambulatory around the central nave. The building's dimensions were noteworthy – 65 meters in length and 23 in width. The central nave was 13 meters wide and about 13.80 meters high; its light filtered through a series of large centered arch windows, and it was separated from the side aisles (6.50 meters wide and about 6.80 meters high) by a row of pillars, rectangular in section, with connecting arches. The wall painting was marbled and there was no floor – the ground was completely covered with tombs. The entrance was in the south wall of the narthex, which was encompassed by the naves after the imperial mausoleum had been built to the east. Standing before the mausoleum was an atrium, 28.40 meters long and 9.50 meters wide. It had three large openings communicating with the adjoining basilica. The mausoleum itself was over 25 meters high and had a circular plan

80

with a diameter of 27.74 meters outside and 20.18 inside. It was illuminated by a series of large arch windows and was covered by a low, flattened dome. In the walls were seven niches, alternately semicircular and rectangular. The one on an axis with the basilica was destined for the imperial sarcophagus. Many other mausoleums were part of the complex, some of them isolated, others backing against the south wall of the basilica, and still others either inside or backed up against the rectangular porticoes which were connected to the basilica's north and south sides at the height of the apse and narthex. But of all these, only the mausoleum of Tiburtius has survived. The basilica is

dated at about 320, and the mausoleum of St. Helen between 324 and 326. The portico is earlier than either. The catacomb frescoes, dated between the third and fourth centuries, illustrate stories from the Old and New Testaments. On the vault of one of the cubicula discovered during the excavations of 1913-15 is a mid third-century cycle of stories of Jonah (Jonah 1, 2). At the center of the vault is the Good Shepherd and all around, alternating with praying figures, is Jonah thrown to the whale, Jonah at rest, and Jonah vomited out of the whale. The fourth episode of the series has been destroyed. In another cubiculum the frescoed episode of Noah and the dove (Genesis 8, 11) shows the patriarch coming out of the ark in an attitude of prayer; on the left, the dove arrives with an olive branch in its beak. The chamber of Niceforus, another discovery of the excavations of 1913-15 named

80. Christ and the woman who had an issue of blood for twelve years. Catacomb of Saints Marcellinus and Peter. This lunette also has two other scenes: the Samaritan woman at the well, and the healing of the lame woman. In the vault is a female figure at prayer. This was unquestionably a woman's tomb.

81

after its probable owner, has in the rear lunette of the arcosolium a fresco of the miracle of the woman who had an issue of blood twelve years (Mark 5, 25-35; Luke 8, 43-48) and, having touched the garment of Jesus, was healed of it. On the left the woman presses forward to touch the Savior's clothes, while Christ, on the right, turns about in surprise at the unexpected touch. Some date the painting midthird-century, others later, between 325 and 350. The tomb called the "Den of Daniel" takes its name from the biblical episode (Daniel 6, 16-24) illustrated on one of its walls. At the center is the young and beardless prophet, his hands raised in a gesture of prayer, identified by the script above his head. Two lions at his sides, each with a paw raised, draw back before him. According to Father Ferrua, who discovered it during the excavations of 1958, this fresco should be dated at the end of the third century. In the recently restored tomb known as the "Chamber of the Four Seasons", a cycle of frescoes with four biblical stories surrounds the entrance door. They include the miracle of the loaves and the fishes, Job, Noah in the ark, and Moses bringing forth water from the rock. The last scene (Exodus 17, 6) is depicted beside the story of Noah and like it prefigures the Baptism. Moses, bearded

and dressed in pallium and sandals, smites the rock with the long rod in his right hand. The image of the prophet resembles that of a Greek philosopher, and probably derives from a classical prototype. Some date it during the latter half of the third century, others between 325 and 350. The chamber is not far from Niceforus's and it, too, was discovered during the excavations of 1913-15.

Another baptism illustration appears in a fresco dating from the first half of the fourth century. It depicts the baptism of Christ (Matthew 3, 14-17; Mark 1, 9-11; Luke 3, 21-22; John 1, 32-33). The Redeemer is shown at the center, youthful and beardless, his feet immersed in the waters of the Jordan. Above, to the left is the dove symbolizing the Holy Ghost, with a series of rays bursting forth from its beak in a shower upon the figure of Christ. Nothing remains of the figure of the Baptist on the right but a hand, firmly placed on the head of the Savior.

On the vault of another chamber is a scene depicting Original Sin (Genesis 3, 7). Adam and Eve, naked, are shown covering themselves with two large fig-leaves, while Eve indicates the forbidden tree with the serpent, her tempter, still wound about it. Another tree on the left serves the scene as stage set. This fresco also dates from the first half of the fourth century.

In the vault of the crypt, which was once believed to contain the bodies of the martyrs of the catacomb, there is a late fourth-century painting, probably deriving from a

81. Jonah thrown to the whale. Catacomb of Saints Marcellinus and Peter.

82

contemporary apse mosaic, divided into two tiers. Above is a bearded, haloed Christ seated on a backless throne, with St. Peter and St. Paul at his side, in accordance with traditional iconography. Below, in the center, the Mystical Lamb is standing upon a hill from which the four rivers of Paradise issue. To the side are the saints, Gorgonius, Peter, Marcellinus and Tiburtius. Garlands of flowers decorate the bottom of the fresco.

82. Noah and the dove. Catacomb of Saints Marcellinus and Peter. The flood is illustrated here with great simplicity. In the biblical scenes decorating the catacombs of the church community, only the easily understandable symbolic meaning was accentuated. In this painting the dead are wished a sure delivery from danger.

83

83. Moses bringing forth water from the rock. Catacomb of Saints Marcellinus and Peter.

84. Canopy cubiculum. Catacomb of Saints Marcellinus and Peter.

85. Original Sin. Catacomb of Saints Marcellinus and Peter.

COEMETERIUM MAIUS

This cemetery, not far from the basilica of Sant'Agnese, has its entrance at 6 Via dell'Asmara. It is called "*maius*" or "greater" maybe to distinguish it from the Minor Cemetery in Via Asmana at number 222. The name is ancient. It appears in St. Jerome's Martyrology, a compilation of testimonies on the lives of the martyrs – though, because St. Emerenziana, foster sister of St. Agnes, is buried here, the catacomb is often called by her name. The martyrs Papia, Alexander, Felix, Maurus and Victor lie here as well. The catacomb, quite long, stretches out on two

86. Lunette with the Madonna and Child. Coemeterium Maius.

levels, and has an underground basilica of sorts and numerous crypts planned for *refrigeria* or funeral banquets. These are decorated with third- and fourth century frescoes, and provided with chairs hollowed out of the tufa, thirteen of which have been found. In addition to Old Testament episodes, the frescoes illustrate such themes as Christ giving his blessing, the faithful at prayer, and the Good Shepherd.

One of the more interesting crypts was erroneously believed to be the place where St. Emerenziana was buried about the middle of the third century. It too has a chair, which in the nineteenth century was thought to have some connection with St. Peter. In the lunette of the arcosolium of an early fourth-century chapel, not far from the actual crypt of St. Emerenziana, is a painting which represents a veiled woman, richly clothed, her hands raised

86

in a prayerful gesture; before her is a child, but only its head with two Constantinian monograms at the sides has survived. Some interpret this image as a representation of the deceased woman with her child. Others see in it the Virgin and Child, but portrayed with an iconography new to third-century catacomb painting. Ordinarily, the Madonna was shown as a full-length figure, seated, with the baby in her lap, and there were nearly always other figures around her – people at prayer and Old Testament characters.

But here only the bust of the female figure is shown, and she is alone with the child. At the borders of the lunette are two praying figures, one male and one female.

The much smaller, near-by Minor Cemetery is not accessible today due to numerous landslips, while the Maius has been the object of constant study and research since the last

century. In fact, its funeral dwellings are architecturally quite elegant, its epigraphs engraved with great precision, and its walls richly decorated with frescoes. Here, a martyr's tomb was discovered there, in a great staircase. But researchers have not been able to identify the inhabitant of this highly atypical underground shrine, for the Maius Cemetery martyrs are distinguished by a singular characteristic: they always appear as a liturgical group in pictures, epigraphs and documents, because in ancient celebrations in their honor, they were all commemorated together. As a result, finding out which of the martyrs is buried in any one of the frescoed or engraved tombs is a very difficult undertaking indeed. It seems that the crypt named after St. Emerenziana contains the remains of the martyrs, Victor and Alexander.

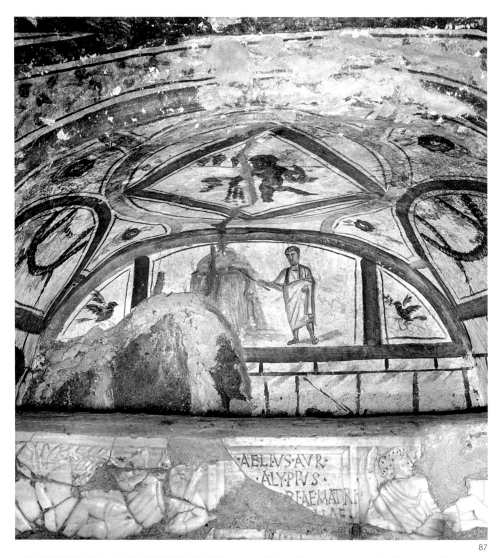

87

ANONYMOUS CEMETERY IN VIA ANAPO

This is one of the Via Salaria cemeteries, but its entrance is between numbers 2 and 4 of Via Anapo. De Rossi held it to be the cemetery of the Giordani, the most famous of the burial sites of Via Salaria and eclipsed only by the Catacomb of Priscilla, but recent findings indicate that it is another private cemetery. The discovery of the original entrance was made accidentally, in 1921, and published by Enrico Josi.

In the cemetery are five chambers frescoed with New and Old Testament subjects. The decoration is dated at the second half

87. Arcosolium of sacellum VIII with Moses who brings forth water from the stone. Anonymous cemetery of Via Anapo.

of the third century. In the first chamber, together with paintings of Daniel in the Lion's Den, the Miracle of the Spring, Noah in the Ark, a praying figure and the Good Shepherd, there is an illustration of the Miracle of the Loaves and Fishes (Matthew 14, 13-21; Mark 6, 30-44; Luke 9, 10-17; John 6, 1-15). Jesus is a youthful, beardless figure, clothed in tunic and pallium, seen extending the long, miracle-working rod resembling Moses' rod towards the seven baskets of bread. Another fresco in the first chamber shows the Resurrection of Lazarus, narrated in the Gospel according to St. John (11, 1-46). Christ is on the right, again young, short-haired and beardless (as was usual in third century frescoes), wearing the tunic and pallium. He extends the selfsame rod until it touches the grave of Lazarus, whose body can be seen inside, bound hand and foot with graveclothes.

In the second cubiculum are Jonah cast forth

88

89

into the sea, and Jonah at rest; in the third,
Abraham's sacrifice, the three children in
the fiery furnace, and Christ with the twelve
apostles.

In the last-named panel, which decorates the
ceiling vault, the young Christ is seated in
the center, surrounded by the twelve apostles,
none of whom are distinguished by any
particular symbolical or character traits. All
the figures were incised in the fresh plaster
beforehand. In the fourth and fifth cubicula
the scenes that were illustrated in the first two
chambers reappear – the praying figures, the
stories of Jonah and Noah.

The other catacomb rooms have purely
ornamental decoration, or none at all.

88, 89. The Resurrection of Lazarus. Catacomb of the Giordani.

90. Christ and the twelve apostles. Anonymous cemetery of Via Anapo.

91. Praying figure, about the middle of the fourth century. Catacomb of the Giordani. This fresco is in the tomb of a woman depicted here in an attitude of prayer, with her name GRATA written on the ochre fascia above her head. She wears a long tunic, which has sleeves and a decoration of "clavi" or purple bands. To the sides are a series of scenes of salvation: the Resurrection of Lazarus to the left and, to the right, the Three Hebrews in the Fiery Furnace and Daniel in the Lion's Den.

92. Richly dressed praying figure. Catacomb of the Giordani. The part of the arenarium pit where this fresco is found had already become a cemetery by the end of the third century, as evidenced by a medallion of Numerianus (283-284) which is still in place in the lime which seals the tomb. This painting may have been done later, during the first part of the fourth century. The great precision evident in the facial portrait seems to indicate that an attempt was made to reproduce real physiognomical traits, a rare occurrence in Roman catacomb painting, although it was quite frequent in the catacombs of Naples. In Rome, the praying figure usually stood for the saved soul in general, and had no connection with the deceased individual. In fact, prayerful female figures decorate men's tombs, and men at prayer can be found on the tombs of women. Only on the tombs of children does the figure at prayer frequently appear as a child of the same age as the deceased.

91

CATACOMB OF THE GIORDANI

Identified during excavations in 1966-69, this was previously (from 1720) believed to be the catacomb of Thraso, named thus after its owner. Its entrance is at the corner of Via Salaria and Via Taro, while the true Thraso catacomb entry lies at 1 Via Yser. The name by which it is still known today may come from the proprietors of the area. In the past this cemetery – deepest of all the Roman catacombs, with its five layers of galleries – was also named Villa Massimo. It includes part of a vast *arenarium* pit in which, outside the cemetery lands, the body of Daria, a converted vestal virgin slain during the Valerian persecution (257-58), and that of her husband Crisantus lie buried – at least according to tradition. A sanctuary to them built in the *arenarium* was much worshipped during the Middle Ages. Later, most of the two martyrs' relics were moved to the basilica of Santissimi Apostoli. The same *arenarium* also contained the sepulchre of a boy martyr named Maurus, and in one of its rooms was the painting of two facing figures at prayer, one of which is here reproduced. Above the figures are two stories of Jonah and Moses striking the rock.

93. Bone statue mounted in one of the catacomb loculi. Catacomb of Pamphilus. It was evidently a personal object, and must have been placed on the tomb to enable the members of the dead man's family to recognize it, since it did not have the more usual and costly epigraph. Many tombs, especially the poorer ones, have signs like these for identification.

94. View of a funeral chamber. Catacomb of Pamphilus.

CATACOMB OF PAMPHILUS

Situated in the Via Paisiello section of Via Salaria Vecchia, beside the Church of St. Pamphilus, this catacomb takes its name from a martyr whose story is unknown. According to the *Hieronymic Martyrology* also the martyrs Cirinus and Candidus were buried here as well. It has been known of since 1594, when Antonio Bosio and Pompeo Ugonio visited some of the first level galleries. A new portion was discovered by Giovan Battista De Rossi in 1865, but the most important excavations were directed by Enrico Josi in 1920. The cemetery was composed of an area above ground and a two-storied catacomb with a mezzanine level. The tombs on the second level were found intact, and decorated with a variety of objects, such as ampullae, terracotta lamps, coins, gilded glass and statuettes. The ancient crypt consisted of a double cubiculum with an arcosolium at the back, against which stood an altar originally covered with slabs of pavonazzetto marble and porphyry. To the right of the crypt is another arcosolium with, at its extremities, two chairs hollowed out of the tufa which may have been used for the *refrigerium* rite. On the walls are graffiti with the names of some presbyters, and a marble slab containing an inscription lettered in porphyry. A niche in the adjacent gallery has a seventh-century image of the Madonna with Child, accompanied by the words DEI GENITRIX. Another funeral chamber, dating from the fourth century, has a whole series of geometric-floral frescoes, and the figure of the Good Shepherd shown in a round of the vault.

95

SANT'AGNESE FUORI LE MURA

This great cemetery complex is composed of the basilica of Sant'Agnese fuori le Mura (St. Agnes outside the Walls), the monumental remains of the so-called *Coemeterium Agnetis*, and the Mausoleum of Costantina Augusta (St. Constantia). Under the basilica and in the surrounding area lie the extended galleries of a vast catacomb, known at least from 1526 and systematically excavated during the XIX century. The cemetery is divided into three main networks. Two of them are even older than the buildings of the monumental complex, all of which are Constantinian and were erected, so it seems, on an imperial property. The first network, to the left of the present basilica, is the oldest. It is dated between the end of the second century and the beginning of the third. The second network, which branches out from behind the apse of Sant'Agnese towards the Via Nomentana, dates back to the third and beginning of the fourth centuries. The third network connects the basilica with the Mausoleum of St. Constantia, and is the

most recent, dating from the fourth and fifth centuries. The cubicula of this catacomb are not frescoed, but numerous inscriptions, graffiti and funerary objects have been found in them. The actual basilica of Sant'Agnese is the result of a reconstruction by Pope Honorius (625-38). It stands on the side of a hill sloping down to the north west, towards the valley where Piazza Annibaliano now lies. The apse above faces onto Via Nomentana, while the facade looks down towards the valley. The edifice is partly built into the hillside, cutting into the galleries of the pre-existing catacomb. In fact, the ground floor is in direct contact with it – or rather, to be precise, with the tomb of St. Agnes, who some believe was martyred during Decius' third-century persecution or Valerian, according to others, martyred during the years of Diocletian (303-304). The upper story, with galleries running above the side aisles and the narthex, has a small bridge in the area of the apse which communicates with Via Nomentana. The basilica of Honorius' time stands on the site of a *sacellum* (or shrine) almost entirely buried in the side of the hill. This was erected simultaneously with the Constantinian basilica, as an altar over the tomb of the saint, and its level has been located at about 0.65 meters beneath the present choir. This first *ad corpus* sacellum was transformed into a small basilica during the fifth century. About thirty meters

95. St. Agnes between two popes, apse dome. Sant'Agnese fuori le Mura.

to the south of the *ad corpus* sacellum stood the so-called *Coemeterium Agnetis*, a large circus-shaped edifice, 98.30 meters long, 40.30 meters wide and over 17 meters high. Of this, there are only the ruins of the south perimetrical wall and of the deambulatory in which it ended to the west. This structure – with robust buttresses reinforcing its walls, pierced by large rectangular windows – is none other than the great cemetery basilica built by order of Constantina, daughter of Constantine, during her widow's years of residence in Rome (338-50), and dedicated by her to St. Agnes. Constantina's building had an atrium in front of it, a large central nave – 80 meters long and 17.50 wide – and 9-meter-wide side aisles linked by a continuous deambulatory in the apse area. In the choir are the remains of a hall with an apse (15 meters by 5.70), but its purpose is unknown. It is also unclear what supporting structures divided the central nave from the side aisles, whether columns, pillars or pilasters; but the building was covered with a truss roof and it certainly had no flooring, for the ground inside was entirely paved with tombs. Other similar structures are the *Basilica Apostolorum* – today's San Sebastiano, the Basilica of Sand Marcellino e Pietro and that of San Lorenzo, all of them cemetery basilicas or *coemeteria subteglata*, literally sheltered cemeteries, destined for funeral ceremonies and especially for the *refrigeria* rites. Judging from documents, the *Coemeterium Agnetis*, unlike the others, seems to have been supplied with a baptistery, perhaps as early as Constantinian times, but certainly by the fifth century. There was an entry to the great mausoleum named for St. Constantia at a point in the south aisle of the basilica somewhat beyond the facade wall. The mausoleum was erected in about 350 as a sepulchre for the bodies of the daughter of Constantine and of her sister, Helen. It is a circular building, and originally had a surrounding portico, a rectangular atrium in front of it, and two apses at its sides. Twelve double columns with composite capitals and connecting arches divided the interior into two concentric areas. The ring-shaped outer area is 22.50 meters in diameter and has a barrel vaulted ceiling with mosaic decorations. One of these represents a scene of pagan derivation, with youths harvesting, carrying and pressing grapes: the theme is profane, but the sense is clearly Christian, and probably refers to the Gospel passage (John 15, 1-17) in which Christ compares himself to the vine and his disciples to the branches. Three large niches were hollowed out of the perimeter wall, and in the one that faced the entrance lay the sarcophagus of St. Constantia, now displayed in the Vatican Museum. The side niches are decorated with two much-restored mosaics showing the *traditio legis* and *the traditio clavium*. The central room, 11.33 meters in diameter and 19 meters high, had a hemispherical cupola supported by a high drum, which was pierced by ample arch windows.

96

96. Plan of the complex of monuments of St. Agnes. The basilica of Honorius, the Mausoleum of St. Constantia, and the still-existent structures of the Constantinian basilica are all indicated. The rectory of Pius IX, and the stairway leading down from it to the level of Honorius' basilica, are shown in black. Visible at the center of the large circusshaped basilica – a typical Constantinian structure – is the small sanctuary discovered during excavations in 1954. Shrines of this sort are not ordinarily found in circus-shaped basilicas – the basilica of Saint Marcellinus and Peter, the basilica of San Lorenzo, etc. – unless they are devotional tombs or areas reserved for funeral banquets (from Perrotti).

Mausoleum of St. Constantia

Constantinian Basilica

Basilica of Honorius

Via di S. Agnese

97

98

97. Apse, St. Constantia.

98. Mosaic with the grape harvest. Mausoleum of St. Constantia.

99. Sarcophagus of St. Constantia, in the Pio-Clementine Museum in the Vatican.

100. View of the interior. Mausoleum of St. Constantia.

SAN PAOLO FUORI LE MURA

The basilica of San Paolo fuori le Mura
(St. Paul's outside the Walls) stands on Via
Ostiense, two kilometers from the Aurelian
Walls and the Porta San Paolo. The present
edifice is a reconstruction (1825-54) of the
building destroyed in the fire of 1823. It has
maintained the design, the dimensions and,
in part, the surviving structures of the older
church. The quadriporticus on its west front
was built *ex novo* between 1890 and 1928.
In pre-Theodosian times, perhaps under

101. Interior of the basilica
of San Paolo fuori le mura.

Constantine, there was another small basilica
on this site, built over a first or second
century monument, which was the tomb and
commemorative monument of the apostle
Paul. The ruins of the apse, brought to light
during the excavations of 1850, show that
its orientation was the reverse of that of the
present church. In 384, or perhaps 386, on
the same site, the three reigning emperors,
Theodosius I, Valentinian II and Arcadius
began the construction of a new, large basilica,
which was finished under Honorius in 395.
The new basilica was created to give the
tomb of St. Paul a monumental setting, as
had been done in Constantinian times with
the basilica of S. Peter which was, in many
ways, its prototype. In front of the edifice on
Via Ostiense was a large porticoed courtyard.
Inside, five aisles separated by columns with

101

connecting arches led to the transept, which was continuous, as in St. Peter's, and slightly projecting beyond the outer walls of the side aisles. The apse to its east was stately, wide as the central nave. The *cella memoriae* erected on the sepulchre of St. Paul was not located on the chord of the apse, as was its twin in St. Peter's, but on a spot quite close to the central nave. The column shafts were plundered from other buildings, but the capitals were specially prepared, composite in the central nave, Corinthian in the side aisles. The dimensions of the basilica were magnificent, surpassing those of all the other basilicas of its time. The breadth of the central nave was 24.22 meters, its length 89.87 meters and its height 30.77 meters. The inner side aisles were 8.96 meters wide and 16.22 meters high, the outer ones, 8.88 meters and 11.65 meters. The depth of

the transept was 24.20 meters, its width 71.01, and its height 26.81. The atrium was 66.80 meters wide and 59.08 meters long. Twenty-one windows flooded light upon the central nave, and the transept was illuminated by twelve arch windows and twelve round ones – but the apse and side aisles had no outside openings.

Not much is known of the original mosaic decoration of the basilica, which was completely redecorated with stucco and frescoes under Leo I (440-61). More important work was done under Gregory I (590-604), who raised the transept level by 90 centimeters and created a new setting for the tomb of St. Paul, building above it, among other things, the principal altar of the basilica. The addition of a baptistery is attributable to Pope Symmachus.

SANTA MARIA MAGGIORE

Towering above the summit of the Esquiline hill is the basilica of Santa Maria Maggiore, dedicated from the first to the "*theotokos*". Its façade is set on the peak of the hill facing south east, and its naves extend north west along an artificial terrace. A series of excavations – some old, some recent – have located the remains of several pre-existing Roman structures below the present building. In the past a connection was thought to exist between Santa Maria Maggiore and the basilica built – according to the *Liber*

Pontificalis – by Pope Liberius (352-66) *iuxta macellum Liviae*. But according to recent studies, there is no link whatsoever between the two buildings. The construction of Santa Maria Maggiore is placed between 400 and 430, and its completion shortly before or during the Pontificate of Sixtus III (432-40), who is credited with having fathered the church. The appearance of the building today is partly the result of restructuring by the architect Ferdinando Fuga between 1741 and 1747, and partly of modifications in the apse area carried out during the Romanesque period. Nevertheless, the aisles still look very

102. Interior of the basilica of Santa Maria Maggiore.

much as they originally did. The fifth-century basilica, like the present one, had three naves, the central one ending in an apse. According to the *Liber Pontificalis* there was a quadriporticus in front, but no traces of this structure have been found. The total width of the building including the perimeter walls was about 35 meters. The central nave, excluding the apse, was 71.56 meters in length, between 17.45 meters and 17.60 meters in width, and 18.35 meters in height at the point where the ceiling began. Then as now it was separated from the aisles by twenty columns on each side. These had bases of varying heights, and

were crowned by Ionic capitals and connected by a classical architrave. Bordering the arch windows above the architrave were pilaster strips with Corinthian capitals, placed in line with the columns below. Beneath the windows, stucco niches framed mosaic panels illustrating Old Testament stories. The apse was originally connected to the triumphal arch and lighted by five large arch windows. All the mosaics in the central nave were done when the church was built, although there is a stylistic difference between those on the side walls and that of the triumphal arch. Stories from Genesis are illustrated on the left wall,

103

stories from Exodus, Numbers and Joshua on the right. Among the latter is a scene believed to represent Moses as a young boy adopted by the Pharaoh's daughter (Exodus 11, 4-10). The princess is seated on a small throne with a tympanum, on the left. The

103. Mosaic with Moses handed over to the Pharaoh's daughter. Santa Maria Maggiore.

maiden pushing the child has been identified as Moses' sister, and the woman holding the basket of fruit on the far right as his mother. In the lower part of the same panel, Moses is shown in discussion with the wise men of Egypt. Another scene illustrated on the right wall of the central nave shows Joshua leading the Jews across the Jordan (Joshua 3, 15-17). Below, the same panel depicts the Jewish warrior sending two spies to Jericho (Joshua 2, 1). Some believe that the mosaics of the triumphal arch celebrate the advent of the Savior and the sovereignty of Christ; for others the subject is the Council of Ephesus (431), which proclaimed the dogma of Mary's divine motherhood. The mosaic artists, with wonderful skill, sought to express this sublime attribute. The Virgin is always accompanied by a retinue of Angels in the evangelical scenes illustrated. All of the episodes regard the infancy of Jesus: after the Annunciation comes the Adoration of the Magi, the Presentation in the Temple, the Flight into Egypt, and the Slaughter of the Innocents.

The cities of Jerusalem and Bethlehem are shown below. At the center of the arch is the Pope's dedicatory inscription, "XISTVS EPISCOPVS PLEBI DEI", meaning: "Built by Sixtus the Bishop for the people of God". The Pope was Sixtus III.

104. The crossing of the Jordan. Santa Maria Maggiore.

SANTA SABINA

The basilica of Santa Sabina, standing at the top of the Aventine hill with one flank facing the Tiber valley, has a south-west/north-east orientation and was built on a series of pre-existing structures, some of them partially encompassed by the new edifice. One of these old structures is the facade of an *insula* type Roman house with a shop on the ground floor, which was incorporated in the perimeter wall of the basilica's south nave. Another, part of a building sometimes identified as the *titulus* of Santa Sabina and extending in the same north-easterly direction as today's church, was used to make up the outer wall of the narthex, to the southwest. The basilica was restored to its early Christian appearance

105. Exterior of the basilica of Santa Sabina.

during the twentieth century.
It was built during the Pontificate of Celestine I (422-32) by a Dalmatian priest, Peter of Illyria, and finished during that of Sixtus III (432-40). The plan is quite simple, with a central nave ending in an apse, and two side aisles. In front of the facade is the narthex that once had two side entrances from the parallel streets flanking the basilica: to the west was the *Vicus Altus* entry, now gone, and to the east that of *Vicus Armilustri*, today Via S. Sabina. Leading to the interior of the church were three doors instead of the present-day two. Altogether, the basilica with the narthex is 62.98 meters long and 24.80 meters wide. Two rows of twenty-four Corinthian columns with connecting arches separate the side aisles from the central nave, which is lighted by a series of ample arch windows set in line with the intercolumn. Three great openings, also with centered arches, illuminate the apse, while the windows in the side aisles are smaller. Much of the interior decoration of the fifth century basilica has been lost.

105

An *opus sectile* frieze – the incrustation is of marble – survives in the central nave above the colonnade, and shows a masonry curtain surmounted by a fascia with rounds, squares and rectangles. Aligned with each column is a military insignia, symbol of the triumph of Christ and His faith throughout the Empire. Not a trace remains of the decoration above, but it too may have been in *opus sectile*, a type of inlay in which the pieces are cut into shapes that follow the lines of the pattern or picture. Also in the central nave is a large mosaic fascia inscribed with the church dedication. The Latin text reads: "When Celestine had the supreme apostolic dignity/and shone through all the world as the first of Bishops/ This marvel was created by a priest of Rome, a native of Illyria/Peter, a man worthy of this name for his nourishment from birth was in the wake of Christ/Rich for the poor, poor for himself/Having shunned the good things of the present life/He well deserves to hope for the gift of the future life". To the sides are two female figures, representing

the Church's origins in east and west: on the left, the Synagogue with the book of the Old Testament; on the right, the Church with that of the New. Originally St. Peter and St. Paul and the symbols of the four evangelists were shown above. The wooden door at the entrance to the central nave was probably built at the same time as the basilica. Made of cypress, it is decorated on both sides. The front ornamentation consists of a series of eighteen rectangular panels – there were originally twenty-eight – of which the larger ones are set vertically and the smaller ones horizontally. The whole is framed by a frieze of twisted vine branches with zoological motifs. The panels depict stories of Moses, Elijah and Christ. The entire group is held to be an illustration of St. Augustine's famous comparison of the Law, the Prophets and the Gospels. The iconography suggests oriental, perhaps Syrian, influences and derives from two different kinds of illuminated manuscripts. The source of the large panel compositions is the *rotulus* or illustrated roll

106

miniature, that of the small panel decoration is the *codex* or bound book miniature. The panel with the crucifixion is the oldest sculptural representation of this theme: triumphant over death, a bearded, wide-eyed and halo-less Christ stands between the two robbers; there is a mere hint of the presence of the crosses, and the figures are naked, except for the *subligaculum* round their loins. In the background are three stylized buildings.

Another panel illustrates three of Christ's miracles, all taken from the Gospel according to St. John. The marriage of Cana (2, 1-11) is below; in the center is the miracle of the loaves and fishes (6, 1-15); and above, the healing of the man who was blind from birth (9, 1-33). On the back of the door is a series of floral motifs inspired by the botanical treatise of Dioscorides, an Alexandrian physician of the first century. In 1836 the door was restored.

106. Wooden door: three of Christ's miracles. Santa Sabina.

107. The Crucifixion, wooden door. Santa Sabina.

108. Interior of the basilica of Santa Sabina.

107

108

SANTO STEFANO ROTONDO

The church of Santo Stefano Rotondo, rising
on the slopes of the Cello with its entrance
on Via del Cello, has at various times in the
course of the past centuries been taken for
a temple, a *macellum* – or ancient market –,
and a basilica. It was built by Pope Simplicius
between 468 and 483, and decorated with
mosaics and marble incrustations by Popes
John I and Felix IV between 523 and 530.
Unfortunately the decoration is lost to us
today. Santo Stefano Rotondo had no resident
clergy, and probably depended for them on St.
John Lateran. Although no relic has ever been
found nor the presence of one documented,

the martyr worshipped here was surely St.
Stephen – to whom, after all, the church was
dedicated. The original structure can still be
recognized in the present edifice despite the
ravages of time and the modifications and
restorations of past centuries. The plan consists
of three concentric circular areas enclosed by a
perimeter wall whose diameter is 65.80 meters.
The external area, 10.60 meters wide, suffered
the greatest damage. Originally it was divided
symmetrically into eight sections, four located
at each of the cardinal points and four at the
diagonal to them. There were eight entrances
into the diagonal sections, and they led into
curvilinear covered passageways, parallel to the
outer wall and communicating with the four
radial chapels which occupied the cardinal
sections. In each of the diagonal sections, free
space, towards the interior of the edifice, was
created by the curvilinear entrance passageways,
and in these spaces – perhaps once open-air
courtyards – there were elegant Serlian three-

109

mullioned opening communicating with the radial chapels. The roof over the chapels was higher than that over the diagonal sections, giving the building a cruciform appearance. An arcaded colonnade separated the outer area from the middle one and created a 9.40 meterwide circular nave, communicating with the radial chapels, and receiving light from the courtyards in the diagonal sections. A second circular colonnade of twenty-two Ionic columns with beams above separated the nave in the middle area from the rotunda in the center. The rotunda diameter was 22.50 and its height about the same. Its light came from twenty-two arch windows in the tambour, which supports the roof just under the ceiling

of the nave. These windows – partly obstructed today – were aligned with the intercolumns below. There are no traces of an altar in the rotunda center, and it is possible that it was always in the east chapel, as it is now.

110

110. Cronaca, plan of Santo Stefano Rotondo (Florence, Gabinetto dei Disegni e delle Stampe degli Uffizi).

SANTA PUDENZIANA

The basilica of Santa Pudenziana, located in the valley separating the Esquiline from the Viminal hill, has its facade fronting on Via Urbana, the former *Vicus Patricius*, and its apse on Via Balbo; but its appearance, transformed by century after century of restoration, is no longer that of the basilica built in early Christian times – which was itself the result of the renovation, begun in about 387-90 and completed in about 398, of two pre-existent Roman buildings, a mid-second century house and a thermal building. The

111. Apse mosaic with Christ the Teacher among the Apostles. Basilica of Santa Pudenziana.

house may have been the old *titulus* of Pudens. If so, it would explain why the writing on the book held by the Savior in the apse mosaic refers not to the hypothetical St. Pudenziana or Potentiana, but to an equally hypothetical Roman senator named Pudens, friend to the apostles, who made his home into a church. The same apse mosaic had another inscription, lost to us today. It gave the donors' names – Ilicius, Maximus and Leopardus – and made it possible to date the completion of decorative work on the church, of which the mosaic is the only surviving part, to the period of Pope Innocent I (401-17).

The mosaic shows Christ enthroned in majesty with the apostles, who form a semicircle around Him. He is clothed in purple and holds in his left hand the book inscribed

111

DOMINUS CONSERVATOR ECCLESIAE PUDENTIANAE, while His right is raised in an oratorical gesture. The Savior is represented according to a scheme clearly deriving from the Imperial iconography of Christ the King, which is associated with a theme very common in the fifth century, that of Christ Teaching. To either side of Him are Peter and Paul. Behind them two female figures symbolizing the *ecclesia ex circumcisione* and the *ecclesia ex gentibus* (or Saint Pudentiana and Saint Prassede, according to other scholars) are shown placing crowns on their heads. At the Savior's feet the Mystical Lamb stretches its head towards the dove, symbol of the Holy Ghost. In the background, a curved portico with some buildings rising behind it – among them a rotunda and an octagonal edifice – may very well represent holy places in Palestine. The portico might correspond to the Anastatian church in Jerusalem, and the monuments behind it to the basilica on Golgotha, to the Imbomon on the Mount of Olives, or to the Church of the Nativity in Bethlehem. A great jewelled cross rises on a mound behind the Redeemer. At its sides, in heaven, are the symbols of the four evangelists – eagle, ox, lion and angel. The mosaic has suffered repeated damage, the worst of it during restoration of the church in 1588. Two apostles and the Mystical Lamb are missing. It has also been restored many times over, in the sixteenth and seventeenth centuries in fresco, in the nineteenth in mosaic, and as a result almost the entire right-hand side has been redone: in fact, all that remains of the original is the overall composition scheme and the head of St. Peter.

SANTI COSMA E DAMIANO

The basilica of Santi Cosma e Damiano stands at the edge of the Roman Forum, beside the basilica of Maxentius, with its present-day entrance facing on Via dei Fori Imperiali – the original one was on Via Sacra. Since pre-existing Constantinian civil structures were used to construct the basilica, it cannot initially have been a cult edifice. The rotunda, serving as entrance to the great hall and apse, is Constantinian as well, commonly called the Temple of Romulus. The transformation of the building from civil to religious use

112. Apse mosaic with
Christ and the Saints.
Basilica of Santi Cosma
e Damiano.

took place under Pope Felix IV (526-30), who simply decorated the apse with a mosaic, which is still in its place today. It represents Christ poised upon a ladder of clouds, in golden robes, with the scroll of the Law in His hands. Below, on the banks of the Jordan, the river of redemption, and surrounded by scenery not terrestrial, but rather suggesting Paradise, St. Peter and St. Paul present to the Savior the two titular saints of the church, St. Cosmas and St. Damian, in whose veiled hands are the crowns which symbolize their martyrdom. The scene is completed by the back-ground figures of the donor, Felix IV, and St. Theodore, both identified in script, and two palms symbolizing resurrection. In the fascia below, the Mystical Lamb, symbol of Christ, is shown beside twelve sheep, representing the twelve apostles. The general

112

theme of the mosaic is the *Maiestas Domini*. Its representation, linked to the apocalyptic theme of Christ the Judge appearing on Judgment Day, was to become very popular during the Middle Ages, albeit with a different iconography.

In this typically Roman form, typical also of Latium, the reference is to the following Gospel text (Matthew 24, 30) "And then... they shall see the Son of man coming in the clouds of heaven with power and great glory". Over the centuries the mosaic has suffered great damage, and repeated restoration, especially during the sixteenth and seventeenth centuries.

The renewed portions include the entire left-hand area with Felix IV and the lower part of the figure of St. Cosmas beside it, as well as part of the figure of Christ, and the upper area of the half dome with the hand of the Eternal Father. Felix IV is a seventeenth century reconstruction – and probably a faithful one – of the image destroyed in the sixteenth century when Gregory XIII had it painted over with the figure of St. Gregory the Great. The mosaic on the triumphal arch was completed later, during the Pontificate of Sergius I, between 692 and 701. Here too the theme represented is the apocalypse, but the reference is directly to the Revelation of St. John the Divine (4, 5). At the center, inside a *clipeus* or shield, is the jewelled throne, and upon it sits the Mystical Lamb with the cross. The seven seals lie on the footrest still intact. To the side are the seven jewelled lamps of fire, four angels, and the symbols of the evangelists; below, the twenty-four elders dressed in white raiment raise the crowns on their veiled hands.

113. "Dogmatic" sarcophagus. Pio Christian Museum.

PIO CHRISTIAN MUSEUM

The museum is housed in a new building in the Vatican, erected after 1963 by the Passarelli brothers to contain the collections until then on display in the Lateran Palace, which Pope John XXIII had decided to reappoint the seat of the Vicariate. The collection is essentially that created by Pius IX in 1854, when he entrusted Father Giuseppe Marchi with organization of the sculptures and Giovan Battista De Rossi with that of the inscriptions, though the new arrangement is the work of Enrico Josi, assisted by Father Umberto Fasola. The new museum begins where the Gregorian Profane Museum ends, as a continuation of the same tour. The gallery of Christian sarcophagi, the richest and most important collection of its kind, makes it possible to follow the chronological, iconographical and stylistic evolution of Early

113

Christian sculpture for at least 150 years, until the new custom of burying the dead beneath the floors of cemetery basilicas came to be adopted in Rome. The sarcophagus represented the most luxurious form of burial. It was a rectangular or oval shaped casket covered by a lid, either pitched in two directions like a roof or flat, with a tablet for inscriptions in the center, and with scenes sculpted on lid and sides drawn mainly from the Old and New Testaments. The favored episodes from the latter were miracles showing the Savior's omnipotence – resurrections, healings, and the miracle of the loaves and fishes. Father Marchi put together the Lateran collection by reconstructing the mutilated and truncated sarcophagi in the Christian Museum of the Vatican Library, and by having others transferred from Roman churches, basilicas and catacombs to the new site. In the present display, the sarcophagi still have their old inventory numbers, which, are listed in the Museum catalogue published by J. Ficker in 1894 and in F.W. Deichmann's *Repertorium* of 1967. One inscription, on a gravestone of the first half of the fourth century, has a graffito

114

MVNIFICENTIA.LEONIS.

114. Sarcophagus
of the Three Shepherds.
Pio Christian Museum.

115. Oval or tub-shaped
sarcophagus. Pio Christian
Museum.

115

116

with the name of the owner, Seberus, and a cask on the left representing his trade. In the center, enclosed in a stylized laurel wreath, the monogram of Constantine appears, with the letters of the Apocalypse Ω and A, the end and the beginning, to the side. A particularly interesting sarcophagus with decoration on four sides has, on the front, three shepherds standing on ornamented pedestals, the bearded central figure carrying a ram on his shoulder, the beardless youths on either side of him each with a ewe. They are dressed in short tunics with gaiters and boots, and carry the shepherds crook and knapsack. The surface between these figures is crowded with the representation of a wine harvest, at which winged genii clamber up the vine branches to pick the grapes and place them in a vat for pressing, shown at the bottom

right. At the top, Psyche rushes off towards a resting genie, with a basketful of grapes in her hands; another genie is milking a goat at the bottom left. The decoration of the sides of this sarcophagus, in two tiers, symbolizes the four seasons by illustrating the work that typifies each of them. The back has a transenna-like decoration with scale motifs. The sarcophagus was found in the Vigna Buonfiglioli near the cemetery of Praetextatus, to the left of the Appian Way, and dates from the latter part of the fourth century. Another oval tub-shaped sarcophagus has a sculpture with two crouching rams to the sides and the Good Shepherd in the center between two trees, with a ram on his shoulder and two more at his feet. He is shown turning towards a veiled woman in an attitude of prayer. A second woman beside her is seated, with a scroll in her left hand, and her right hand raised as she converses. On the left, two men in philosopher's dress are engaged in a discussion; the one in the center is seated, and holds in his hands a partly opened scroll. A sun dial can be seen behind. The

116. Gravestone
of Seberus.
Pio Christian Museum.

two seated figures are held to be the couple who commissioned the sarcophagus, which was found in 1881 in Via Salaria, near the mausoleum of Licinius Peto, and purchased by Leo XIII in 1891. Most scholars place it in the period of Gallienus (253-60). The "dogmatic" sarcophagus is so-called because the reliefs on the front, the only side with decoration, are of profoundly religious inspiration. They are arranged in two tiers. Above, from right to left, are: the creation of man and woman by the Holy Trinity; the Savior giving Adam and Eve means of sustenance after the sin; a *Clipeus* with busts of both the deceased (only sketched in); the Miracle of Cana; the Miracle of the loaves and fishes; and the Resurrection of Lazarus. Below, from left to right: the Epiphany; the Healing of the man who was blind from birth; Daniel in the Lion's Den; Christ prophesying to Peter that he should deny Him thrice; and the Capture of St. Paul and St. Peter. The sarcophagus (325-350) was found in 1838 during work on the foundation of the baldachin of San Paolo fuori le Mura,

and is dated latter half of the fourth century. The Epiphany also appears on the right side of the lid of a now fragmentary sarcophagus. On the casket were the Entrance into Jerusalem, the Delivery of the Law, and Christ before Pilate. The sarcophagus, from the latter part of the fourth century, comes from the Vatican necropoli. On a gravestone, also from the fourth century, the deceased is portrayed at the center with her arms raised in a gesture of prayer, while a dove presents her with a crown. The inscription ALEXANDRA IN PACE appears at the side. A last sarcophagus represents a youthful Christ dressed as a shepherd with the twelve apostles surrounding him. Twelve sheep lie at their feet. As background to the scene, two young shepherds are shown moving among flocks of sheep and trees. This sarcophagus, of the second half of the fourth century, comes from San Lorenzo fuori le Mura. Completing the collection are a series of casts of particularly important pieces not belonging to the museum, a mosaic portrait of a deceased couple coming from Agro Verano

117

118

117. Fragment of
sarcophagus lid with
Adoration of the Magi.
Pio Christian Museum.

118. The gravestone
of Alexandra.
Pio Christian Museum.

119. Sarcophagus with
Christ and the Apostles.
Pio Christian Museum.

119

and donated by Benedict XV, and a bell from Canino in the province of Viterbo, dating from the eighth century and held to be the oldest example of this instrument. There are also two statues of the Good Shepherd, both accurately following the description in the Gospel passage (Luke 15, 4,5). They portray a curly-haired youth, dressed in a short tunic belted at the waist, with a lamb on his shoulder. In the older statue, dating from the first half of the fourth century, the shepherd has a knapsack slung over his back; the lower part of the tunic and the legs have been restored. The piece was part of the Mariotti collection in the Lateran Museum since the eighteenth century. In the second statue, from the second half of the fourth century, the shepherd holds a gnarled and knotty stick in his hand. The image of the devotee bringing offerings to the temple also occurs in pagan sculpture, in forms similar to this. But these statuettes have a different meaning, and the image clearly refers to Christ, at once shepherd and Lamb (John 10, 11-18). The epigraphical collection created by De Rossi is on display; here, inscriptions of various origin are united in an organic grouping.

The collection includes the inscriptions accumulated in the storage rooms of the Museum and the Vatican Library after the Pontificate of Plus VII, those coming from the excavations at Ostia and from research explorations of the catacombs, those from Agro Verano, donated by the municipality of Rome, and those found by De Rossi in various monasteries, churches and chapels. At a later date the collection was enriched by a group of Hebrew inscriptions. De Rossi divided the material into two groups, classifying one *Inscriptiones sacrae* – a precious source of primary material for the historian of Christianity and its cult monuments during the first centuries –, and the other *Inscriptiones selectae* – a selection of monuments according to their importance. The first group was divided into inscriptions regarding sacred buildings, their revenues and their donations, and inscriptions in praise of the martyrs. The latter was again subdivided into three groups; the first one chronological, containing inscriptions whose dates were certain, until the year 365; the second dogmatic, including epigraphs with formulas which expound and illustrate faith, discipline, ecclesiastical hierarchy, civil conditions, and family; and the third topographical, dividing the material according to the Christian cemeteries of Rome from which it came. De Rossi's classification has been respected, as far as possible, in the present arrangement of the material.

121

120-121. Two sculptures of the Good Shepherd. Pio Christian Museum.

122. Rear lunette of an arcosolium with a pair of doves and garlands of flowers. Catacomb of Pamphilus.

Glossary

AEDICULA. Small building often in the shape of a classical temple, covering a statue or a picture.

ARCOSOLIUM. Sepulchral monument made out of an arch or a sarcophagus, fitted into a niche that generally has a semicircular vault.

BASILICA. Edifice on a longitudinal axis, consisting of a central nave separated from two or four lateral naves by rows of columns. It is endowed with an apse and often an atrium or narthex. Employing a structure originally used by the Romans for civil purposes, the early Christians adopted the basilica plan for the centers of their cult.

CUBICULUM. The bedroom in a Roman house where the children and the servants slept. In the catacombs, it was the crypt or chapel, which opened from the sides of the galleries and contained one or more arcosolia.

DALMATIC. Vestment based on the tunic design, with long sleeves and two strips of red material ornamenting it. It was worn by the Romans until the second century A.D., and thereafter by Christian clergy for liturgical celebrations.

HYPOGEUM. Private underground sepulchre in which deceased persons were entombed. This name was also given to several catacombs.

LOCULI. Long, horizontal cavities hollowed out of the catacomb walls, one atop the other, which held corpses.

MARTYRY. Church constructed over the tomb of a martyr. It can be distinguished from the basilica because it always has a central plan.

MEMORIAL. Sepulchral monument built over the tomb of a martyr or a saint.

NARTHEX. Transverse vestibule preceding the facade of the basilica and consisting of a colonnade or a quadriporticus. Unbaptized Christians were permitted to enter into the narthex.

PALLIUM. Part of the liturgical dress reserved for Papal use, the pallium is a narrow band of white material that hangs down over the wearer's chest.

SACELLUM. Small sepulchre or chapel built over the tomb of a saint or martyr.

TROPHY. Monument over the tomb of a martyr, or on the spot where a martyrdom took place. The name derives from the notion common among the early Christians that a martyrdom was a victory of faith.

Bibliography

J. Wilpert, *Le pitture delle catacombe romane*, Rome 1903.

R. Krautheimer, W. Frankl, S. Corbett, A. Frazer, *Corpus basilicarum Cristianorum Romae, I-V*, Vatican City 1937-1977.

F.W. Deichmann, A. Tschira, *Das Mausoleum der Kaiserin Helena und die Basilika der heiligen Marcellinus und Petrus an der via Labicana von Rom*, in "Jahrbuch des deutschen archäologischen Instituts", LXXII, 1957.

A. Ferrua, *Le pitture della nuova catacomba della via Latina*, Vatican City 1960.

A.P. Frutaz, *Il complesso monumentale di S. Agnese*, Vatican City 1960.

U. Fasola, *La basilica dei Santi Nereo e Achilleo e la catacomba di Domitilla*, Roma 1965.

F.W. Deichmann, *Repertorium der christlich-antiken Sarkophage*, I, Wiesbaden 1967.

A. Nestori, *Repertorio topografico delle pitture delle catacombe romane*, Rome 1975.

U. Fasola, *Pietro e Paolo a Roma. Orme sulla roccia*, Rome 1980.

A. Grabar, *L'arte paleocristiana 200-395*, Milan 1980.

A. Grabar, *L'età d'oro di Giustiniano. Dalla morte di Teodosio all'Islam*, Milano 1980.

S. Carletti, *Guida delle Catacombe di Priscilla*, Vatican City 1981.

A. Ferrua, *La basilica e la catacomba di San Sebastiano*, Vatican City 1990.

A. Ferrua, *Catacombe sconosciute. Una catacomba del IV secolo sotto la via Latina*, Florence 1990.

R. Vicchi, *Le basiliche maggiori di Roma. San Pietro, San Giovanni in Laterano, San Paolo fuori le Mura, Santa Maria Maggiore*, Florence 1999.

G. Spinola, *I sarcofagi paleocristiani del Museo Pio Cristiano ex Lateranense nei Musei Vaticani*, in "Rivista di Archeologia Cristiana", LXXVII, 2001, pp. 545-569.

V. Fiocchi Niccolai, F. Bisconti, D. Mazzoleni, *Le catacombe cristiane di Roma. Origini, sviluppo, apparati decorativi, documentazione epigrafica*, Regensburg 2002.

P. Pergola, *Le catacombe romane. Storia e topografia*, Rome 2002.

U. Brandeburg, *Le prime chiese di Roma IV-VII secolo. L'inizio dell'architetture ecclesiastica occidentale*, Milan 2004.

The illustrations in this publication have been
provided by SCALA ARCHIVES, the most important
source in the world for color photographs and digital
images of the visual arts.
Over 200,000 subjects are availabe for fast and
accurate iconographic research, at all levels, in the
online database.
www.scalarchives.it

e-mail archivio@scalagroup.com

ISBN: 183-88-8117-241-2

Printed by: Grafiche Flaminia, Foligno (PG), 2007